D1202476

Extreme decision making

When Your Life Depends On It

Lessons from the Antarctic

By Brad Borkan and David Hirzel

Copyright © Brad Borkan, David Hirzel 2017

Brad Borkan and David Hirzel have asserted their moral right to be identified
as the authors of this work in accordance with UK and US copyright law.

All rights reserved.
Without limiting the rights under the copyright reserved above,
no part of this publication may be reproduced, stored in, or introduced into
a retrieval system, or transmitted, in any form, or by any means (electronic,
mechanical, photocopying, recording, or otherwise), without the prior
written permission of the authors.

ISBN 978-1-945312-05-2

Terra Nova Press
P. O. Box 1808
Pacifica CA 94044

Cover photograph from the
Scott Polar Research Institute.

Dedication

Although we grew up on opposite coasts of the United States, and ultimately settled on different continents, we realized we had the same sentiment regarding how to dedicate this book:

To Brad's parents,
Jean and Harold Borkan

and

To David's parents,
Edwin F. and Doris Hirzel

By example they taught us to consider carefully, choose wisely, and follow through with decisions large and small.
We hope we have passed this on to future generations.

We hope this book encourages you to read more about these remarkable adventures. See our Recommended Reading List at the back of the book, and our website *www.extreme-decisions.com,* for links to books and videos we think you might enjoy.

To improve readability, we have kept footnotes to a minimum.

The map on page 8 and the tables at the back of the book will be a helpful reference in understanding each expedition's time scales, leaders, ships, huts, key locations, major journeys and personnel.

All distances are in statute miles (5,280 feet), unless otherwise noted. Temperatures are shown in Fahrenheit, which was commonly used during the 1900s.

Contents

Map of Expeditions

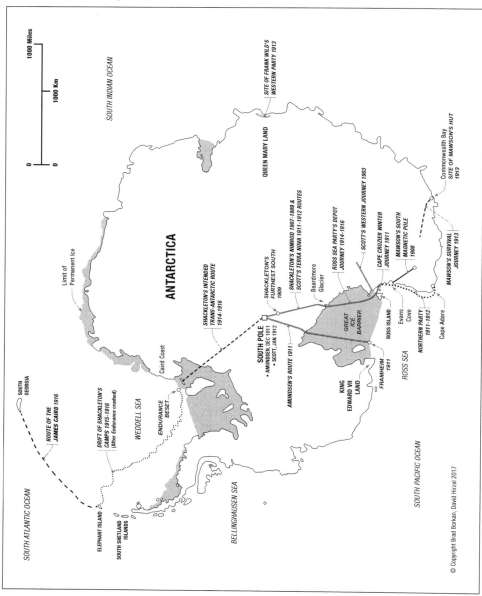

This map shows the relative locations of sites in Antarctica and the paths of the six Antarctic heroic age expeditions cited in this book. Scale is only approximate. A larger version of the map can be found on our website: *www.extreme-decisions.com*.

Foreword

by Dr. David M. Wilson

My great uncle may be known to the world as Dr. Edward Wilson, Antarctic explorer and scientist—a gifted artist; friend of Sir Ernest Shackleton; Chief of Scientific Staff to Captain Robert Scott; and in every respect a pivotal figure in what has become known as the heroic age of Antarctic Exploration. To me, however, he was simply family.

Great-uncle Ted. That's how I knew him when I was growing up in the Wilson household. My grandfather's beloved older brother. I never met my great-uncle—he died in Antarctica on the return from the South Pole in 1912, years before I was born—but I knew my grandfather and remember how he talked of his brother.

Edward Wilson, one of ten children, was born in Cheltenham in the southwest of England, and was a man who loved the natural world and liked nothing better than to explore it. His accomplishments were many. On the *Discovery* Expedition he was part of the three-man team that reached the furthest south in 1902. On the *Terra Nova* Expedition in 1911, he led the Winter Journey in search of penguin eggs, and later was a member of the five-man Polar Party, reaching the South Pole on January 18, 1912.

To give you an idea of what he and his companions endured in the name of science, discovery and exploration, envision this scene from the Winter Journey:

> Great-uncle Ted and his two colleagues were lying inside a small, uninsulated rock-sided shelter *in the middle of an Antarctic winter*, listening to the screaming wind of a blizzard as it raged outside. Suddenly their tent, pitched nearby, blew away; followed a short time later by the roof of their shelter. They were left exposed to the full ferocity of the icy tumult. Death stared them in the face. It was my great uncle's 39th birthday.

> Without shelter they might not survive the night; without a tent, they would surely not survive the trip back. Why even embark on such a life threatening journey in the coldest, darkest part of the year? How did they live to tell the tale and what exactly did they discover? And importantly, what lessons can we learn from this remarkable team that can help with our modern day lives?

This book is a page-turner with true stories that will sear you to the depth of your soul. It brings to life a time when ordinary people faced extraordinary challenges as they pushed forward the boundaries of human knowledge against powerful forces in a hostile environment. The stories and the decision making lessons derived from them will stay with you for the rest of your life.

A treasure trove of epic adventures from the six major Antarctic expeditions from the heroic era, this book has a central focus on the life and death decisions the men made on the ice. My great-uncle Ted was on two of those expeditions. It is only when you realise that all of the people in these stories are normal human beings like you and me that the enormity of what they achieved will astonish you.

The message of this book is clear. You can also rise to the challenges in your life with similar courage. We all have it within us. The stories may be from over a hundred years ago, but the lessons in how to set and achieve goals, face challenges and counter adversity and risk, with teamwork, leadership, sheer grit, and the determination to never ever give up no matter how bad things get are timeless.

Their accomplishments were achieved by flesh and blood, like yours and mine, and so set a benchmark for our lives today. After reading this book you have every chance of making better decisions in your personal and business life. Challenges, adversity and risk? You can learn to take them in your stride just as my great-uncle did.

Dr. David M. Wilson
United Kingdom

January 2017

Antarctic historian and author of The Lost Photographs of Captain Scott: Unseen Images from the Legendary Antarctic Expedition and Cheltenham in Antarctica: The Life of Edward Wilson as well as other books on the heroic age.

It's Your Call

Antarctica—the early 1900s.
The only communication is as far as you can shout.

You and your two companions are nearing the end of a fifteen-hundred-mile trek to a nameless spot on the South Polar Plateau.

To say conditions are harsh would be an understatement. Temperatures can get so low that you risk frostbite even when bundled in your reindeer-hide sleeping bags. The jagged, frozen landscape provides constant challenges, including the danger of crevasses cracking open unexpectedly beneath your feet, plunging you into their depths. At times you have been on the verge of starvation.

Your presence here today is the result of countless decisions great and small made along the way. Right now you are faced with a decision greater than any that came before. One of your companions has fallen so ill with scurvy he can no longer walk.

Seventy miles of dangerous terrain lie ahead before you reach the safety of your base camp, and you will have to drag him on the sledge, adding an almost unbearable weight to that of your ice-encrusted tent and the last remnants of food keeping you alive.

The reality of the situation is grim. You must maintain a steady pace each day, regardless of the weather, to reach the next depot of supplies before those on hand run out. Your daily distances have fallen off, and continue to fall. The sick man, already perilously near death, is unlikely to survive the remainder of the journey.

With his extra weight further reducing your daily mileage, neither will you and your other companion. You all know the fate that lies ahead. The sick man tells the two of you to leave him here on the Barrier and march on ahead with the sledge and supplies, to save yourselves while you can. The three of you have developed a close camaraderie during your long walk; leaving him to perish on the ice is inconceivable. The obvious, ethical, human decision: to shoulder your burden and do your best.

The situation is not so straightforward. You are seamen and the sick man is your commanding officer. He has *commanded* you to leave him behind. The one thing that has been repeatedly drilled into you throughout your entire working life is this: there is *no* occasion on which you can refuse to comply with the order of an officer.

To obey means the two of you have at least a chance at survival; to refuse is mutiny, and certain death for all three of you.

The choice is now yours—it's your call.

How will you decide?

* * *

This was a real event faced by real people. They did have to make this call. Their decision and the outcome may surprise you. You will find the rest of the story later in this book.

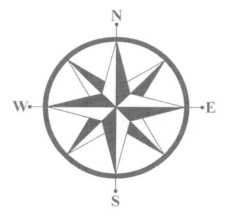

When Your Life Depends On It

Decision making in extreme environments.
It's not like crossing the street.

People make decisions every day, but not like those made by polar explorers in the early 1900s. Yet, there is much that we can learn from their extraordinary stories that can help us make better decisions in our own modern lives.

The early Antarctic explorers were not perfect decision makers. However they were exceptionally good at facing the reality of every situation, taking choices as they arose, and even if they did not make an ideal decision, making the very best of whatever situation they found themselves in.

They set and achieved monumental goals in an extreme environment. They did this while encountering jaw-dropping amounts of adversity and risk which they overcame through teamwork, leadership, and sheer grit and determination. It is the example of these explorers' methods—pragmatic, simple, and, quite literally, down to earth—that can instruct and guide us in our life and business choices.

Our decisions may not be as world-shaking and dramatic, but using these stories as inspiration, there is much that can be learned from considering their situations and the decisions they made—

lessons that can positively influence how we lead our lives today. Antarctica was once a vast *terra incognita*. Its continental nature was only suspected from isolated sightings of a shoreline guarded by wide belts of pack ice, with a perimeter roughly defined by the Antarctic Circle. Once within that pack ice, and landed on that shore, there could be no help expected from the outside world.

Polar exploration up until the 1920s was largely done overland on foot, before the era of mechanized travel and reliable radio communication. The explorers travelled to the polar regions in wooden ships and were left on shore with a supply of stores and only their own willpower, strength, intelligence and, dare we say, luck to carry through their objectives. Every possible need and circumstance had to be anticipated and preplanned using a limited store of knowledge dating as far back as Captain Cook in the 1700s.

Some decisions were made before departure from the comfort of their home ports. Others, and certainly the most interesting and compelling ones, had to be made after landing on these desolate shores, and later venturing inland, with a desire for science and discovery, and a quest to be the first to the South Pole.

These early explorers faced the most awe-inspiring, gut-wrenchingly difficult decisions—often with life or death in the balance—with grace, determination, and even nobility. The results of their decisions were mixed. Some were good; others made dire circumstances even more hazardous. Regardless of the outcome, the stories of *how* they faced these decisions are unforgettable. The lessons derived from them are as important today as they were one hundred years ago.

Examples of some of the lessons include:

1. They met every decision head-on, and made the best of a bad decision.

2. Large and small teams were led effectively, but as you will see, leadership on the early expeditions adapted to situations as needed. Not every leader succeeded every time and often small teams had either a designated or an unspoken second-in-command who could rise to the challenge when needed.

3. They sought and found inspiration when needed from a variety of sources.

4. Despite endless amounts of adversity, they never ever gave up hope, courage, determination and teamwork.

5. They discovered that sometimes when fate had a way of preventing them from achieving one goal, it also gave opportunities to achieve a different one, which might even become more significant.

6. Within ourselves we have untapped mental and physical strength—far more than we might think we have.

7. They proved that when all else fails, bad luck descends, and the end is truly in sight, that we have the capacity within ourselves to act nobly—that when you run out of choices, success might be reframed as simply doing the right thing.

Life and death decisions in the Antarctic

This book examines many of the harrowing polar decisions made by the British, Irish, Australian and Norwegian explorers across six major expeditions between 1901 and 1917. These years have come to be known as the heroic age of Antarctic exploration. The expeditions are listed in the table on page 20.

Their leaders, Robert Scott, Ernest Shackleton, Roald Amundsen, and Douglas Mawson, were ably seconded by men like Lt. Edward "Teddy" Evans, Frank Wild, Aeneas Mackintosh, Thorvald Nilsen, Edward Wilson, and others too numerous to name here.

In looking deeper into the polar decisions made on these expeditions, we found that many of them were well thought out,

British, Norwegian and Australian heroic age expeditions featured in this book

Expedition Name	Dates	Ship	Nationality	Leader	Objectives
Discovery Expedition *Official Name:* British National Antarctic Expedition	1901-1904	*Discovery*	British	Scott	Science, discovery and exploration
Nimrod Expedition *Official Name:* British Antarctic Expedition	1907-1909	*Nimrod*	British	Shackleton	Be first to the South Pole, as well as science and exploration
Terra Nova Expedition *Official Name:* British Antarctic Expedition	1910-1913	*Terra Nova*	British	Scott	Science, exploration and be the first to the South Pole
Norwegian Antarctic Expedition	1910-1912	*Fram*	Norwegian	Amundsen	Race Scott to the South Pole
Australian Antarctic Expedition	1911-1914	*Aurora*	Australian	Mawson	Science, discovery and exploration of 2,000 mile coast of Antarctica
Endurance Expedition *Official Name:* Imperial Trans-Antarctic Expedition	1914-1917	Weddell Sea side: *Endurance* Ross Sea side: *Aurora*	British	Weddell Sea side: Shackleton Ross Sea side: Mackintosh	Be first to cross the Antarctic continent via the South Pole

with due consideration for the people involved and the consequences to be faced. Some were arguably among the most difficult anyone would ever have to make, with life and death consequences for both the individual decision maker himself (all these early polar explorers were men) as well as others on the expeditions.

The challenge was even greater because the outcome of any decision, right or wrong, would rarely be known instantly, but instead played out over many days in a hostile, frozen terrain. If wrong, recovery would not be as simple as a modern life and death decision like "swerve back into your driving lane." An incorrect choice could result in prolonged suffering: scurvy, exhaustion, frozen limbs, snow blindness, and a cold painful death by exposure and starvation.

Our goal in sharing these stories is to help you improve your own decision making and to provide new strategies for dealing with risk and adversity. As will be seen in the expedition stories that run throughout this book, these men set goals, they took risks, and they achieved successes, each in their own way. But most important of all, they made truly heroic decisions in the face of real adversity and, whatever the outcome, accepted the result as simply the next challenge.

How does this relate to modern life?

In modern life, we give scant thought to low-probability risk. We step off a curb, ride a bicycle, drive perhaps faster than we should, take a train, and do a myriad of other things with associated dangers.

This type of risk is minimal for a number of reasons. First, it is familiar. We've taken these risks hundreds or thousands of times before, and seen others do the same without consequence. We learn how to make some of the more complex decisions gradually, by using training wheels on a bicycle, for example, or by taking driving lessons. There are built-in decision support systems such as lines on the roads and crossing lights. These are "controlled" decisions, where we determine the action, timing and potential results.

Modern life also throws "uncontrolled" decisions at us, such as a car accident, but the majority of these at least have predictable patterns. Laws, values, religious beliefs, societal customs and other support systems help us deal with them. When faced with an uncontrolled event, we often know instinctively when to summon the police, a doctor, a relative, or a religious advisor, and when to handle it ourselves.

An uncontrollable world

In contrast, during the heroic age of Antarctic exploration of the early 1900s, even the controlled decisions were met with uncontrollable circumstances. Expeditions were cut off from the world and decision making was done in complete isolation. In an emergency, a call for help traveled only as far as one could shout. There were no lines on these roads, no rule of law and, with no advanced communications equipment, absolutely no means of contacting the outside world.

Once landed, the expeditions were totally self-sufficient and this is what makes the Antarctic such a unique environment in which to analyse decisions. No emergency rescue could be brought in, and there was no one to call on for impartial advice. Not only because there was no communications equipment, but even if there had been, no one could give useful advice. No one had *ever* been where they were standing.

To complicate matters further, nothing was to be found there except snow, ice, and wind. There were no trees to provide wood for fuel, no plants to eat, and no simple way to melt the all-encompassing ice into fresh drinking water. A few species of seals, penguins and other birds had adapted to that environment, but they only lived along the coastlines. On the very first expeditions, explorers couldn't even raid the stores or huts left by those who had come before.

The nearest outpost of civilization was thousands of miles away over the frozen and tempestuous ocean. Once they moved away from the shore, Scott, Shackleton, Amundsen and Mawson, the expedition leaders in this heroic age, could not call in reserves. Whatever they needed, they had to create from what they had brought with them, or do without. Everything had to be well planned from the start and well executed throughout, but as you will see, sometimes even the most careful preparations could come to naught.

Polar decision making has another element to contend with that sets it apart. The extreme cold can hamper one's cognitive ability. It can also be lethal. As little as three minutes of exposure in Antarctic polar conditions can result in frostbite of bare skin. Longer exposure can cause damage so severe that it requires amputation. Unlike an enemy army to be engaged in battle for a period of time, advancing and retreating, the bitter Antarctic cold is ever-present. Twenty-four hours a day, seven days a week for the duration of their time in Antarctica, explorers faced an unrelentingly ruthless, energy-sapping, mind-numbing enemy.

In this regard, polar exploration is more akin to mountain climbing. Mountain ascents like the early assaults of Everest, can be measured in months or weeks, but early Antarctic expeditions left their exploring and scientific parties to fend for themselves for the better part of a year, and often two or three. This span of time added to the hardship and isolation.

Each additional year on the ice meant the entire expedition had to survive another polar winter. From April to September the sun may only barely rise above the horizon, and depending upon how far south one was the sun may not rise *at all* for weeks or months at a time. Temperatures dropped as low as -77°F (-60.5°C). With these extremes, it is easy to imagine how men's tempers could be frayed due to lack of sunlight and warmth. Add multi-day blizzards to the mix, and even a trip from the hut to the latrine could be a perilous journey.

There are many books about the individual Antarctic expeditions that describe in detail their provisioning, ship and crew selection, and other criteria related to pre-expedition decisions. These are all fascinating topics, as are the many common decisions that were made once the expeditions were under way—routine choices of how far to travel each day, when to pitch the tent, how much food to cook at each meal, and so on. Our focus here, however, is on the extremely difficult decision making, where lives literally hung in the balance.

What would you have done?

The next eleven chapters (their titles are listed below) focus on the many polar decisions that the expedition leaders, small groups of explorers, or individual team members made during the heroic age.

- How strong is your will to survive?
- What do you do when luck runs out?
- How well have you prepared?
- Who is in charge?
- Who is on your team?
- Three biscuits and thirty-five miles to go.
- Promises, promises.
- Do you agree all is fair in love, war and polar exploration?
- Will the results be worth the effort?
- All or nothing: When do you take the big risk?
- What is your higher purpose?

As you read further, imagine yourself in their situations. Would you have made the same or different decisions? Where would you draw the line at risk versus reward? What level of risk would you accept to achieve *your* goals? And, most important of all, why did you choose to be there in the first place?

What happened to each of the expeditions will be revealed through the chapters. At the end is a summary of the lessons derived from their decision making that can help with one's own decision making. After all, you may not be holding onto a rope down an icy, frozen crevasse in the Antarctic in the early 1900s, but sometimes modern life can seem that way.

With that as a starting point, let's begin with the one of the toughest decisions of all: How strong is your will to survive, and what would you do if you found yourself in that crevasse?

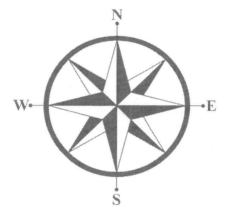

How Strong Is Your Will To Survive?

Where does inspiration come from?

End of the rope.
Imagine that you have spent years planning one of the most ambitious undertakings in Antarctica. Your goal: map and scientifically explore two thousand miles (3,200 km) of unexplored coast. The year: 1912

You assemble a first-class team and manage all the challenges of getting the expedition underway, including fundraising, buying a ship, selecting the scientists and other personnel, as well as acquiring the necessary scientific equipment and provisions.

Once stationed in Antarctica, you divide your twenty-four men into eight sets of three-man teams to explore different regions. There is a clear deadline when the ship will return to Antarctica to pick you and your men up the following year. If you have not made it back to the base camp in time, the ship will depart without you; it will be too dangerous for the ship and crew to wait around for you. Doing so risks everyone on the ship having to stay through another very dark, very cold, very depressing Antarctic winter, and adds to the risk of the ship becoming iced in and crushed.

Your own three-man team is highly accomplished. Xavier Mertz is a 29-year-old Swiss ski champion, and Belgrave Ninnis is a 25-year-old British soldier from the Royal Fusiliers. Your own experience already includes a thousand-mile Antarctic sledge journey. On an earlier expedition, a team had reached the South Magnetic Pole. Now your objective is to locate that elusive point again, this time from another direction, mapping the interior of the continent along the way.

The gear for the three of you, on this seven-hundred-mile roundtrip, is divided between two sledges, but not equally. When crossing fields of concealed crevasses, where the greatest danger lies, one sledge is always pulled at a safe distance behind the first. That second sledge contains the items *most* important for survival— the only tent, most of the food, and the food for the sledge dogs.

But bad luck does happen, even when the planning is good. Two hundred miles (321 km) out along the trail, Ninnis, leading the dogs of the second sledge, must not have seen your warning signal. When you and Mertz stop and look behind, you see to your complete horror that Ninnis, the dogs, and the sledge are gone. Only a hole through a thin snow lid reveals what must have happened. The crevasse is hundreds of feet deep, and they have all plunged into its silent depths.

You and Mertz look at each other. You are stranded. No one knows the tragedy that has befallen you, or the struggle you are about to face on your crippled expedition, as you turn for home.

You will have to recover from the death of your companion, and improvise a way back to your base at Commonwealth Bay, the most windswept part of Antarctica. It is going to be a long tough march. With only a cloth oversheet propped up on ski poles for a makeshift tent, no ground cloth between your sleeping bags and the snow, and with much of your food and most of your sledge dogs lost in the crevasse, you begin the long overland trek back to safety. Now it is day after day of walking, camping, walking, and camping. Progress is slow; food must be carefully rationed. You and Mertz will have to feed on the meat of each dog as it dies.

The dog livers that you relish for their concentrated nutrition bear a hidden menace—lethally high amounts of vitamin A. While still one hundred miles (160 km) out from base camp, Mertz succumbs to the ordeal, and loses his mental capacities. You tie him onto the sledge and drag him forward, but you too are weakened. Your progress is so slow; the two of you may never get back alive. Two days later, Mertz dies. Your meagre supply of food will last only a little longer, but now you can cover more ground in each day's march. Traveling as fast as you are able, you are still likely to miss reaching the coast in time to catch the ship home. The timing is incredibly tight. Even if you do not survive, the closer you get the more likely your records will be found.

You pull yourself together and continue onward. After a few more days of travel on your own, in your weary, starving, and dilapidated state, you fall down a crevasse. The only thing saving you from certain death is the rope of your harness, still attached to your sledge. In a rare bit of good luck, the sledge is wedged in place on the surface, but you are dangling between the blue walls of ice, literally at the end of your rope. There is a knot along the length of the rope, but you are too far from the ice walls to get a foothold to help you get a start. Think back to your school days. Climbing hand-over-hand on a fourteen-foot rope in a warm gymnasium wearing lightweight clothing was difficult. Really difficult. Now imagine doing this in Antarctic winter clothing made in the 1900s. There was no lightweight thinsulate then. Your clothing is soaked from sweat and snow, and you are wearing heavy gloves and heavy boots. And before you envision climbing that rope, think about your two comrades who have died. Add to that these images: even if you make it up the rope, you still have to haul yourself up over the icy rim of the crevasse; if you succeed in that, you still have almost no food. You are physically falling apart due to poor nutrition and the devastating poison of vitamin A. You may not make it to the base camp in time to get the ship. Why not just give up?

One more try

With all the strength you can summon, you climb hand-over-hand up the rope to the crumbling rim. Success!

Well, not quite. As you try to climb over the edge of the crevasse, the ice crumbles away. You fall back down into the crevasse, saved once again by your fourteen-foot rope harness. Now what? With no strength left, do you give up and die? Cut the rope? Unclip the harness? Cry? Curse?

Douglas Mawson could have done any of these things. Instead, he did something different. He remembered a poem.

> Just have one more try
> It's dead easy to die,
> It's the keeping-on-living that's hard.[1]

Think about that. Bad luck, after bad luck, followed by more bad luck, and this man thinks about . . . a poem? Mawson found an unknown reserve of strength, climbed the rope once again, and this time succeeded. That triumph, however, did not mark the end of his challenges. After several more days of walking in the heavy snow, he made it to base camp only to find he had missed the return ship by *five hours*! He'd now have to survive another Antarctic winter with the added misfortune: where they had built their original base camp had turned out to be the windiest place on Earth clocking speeds of more than two hundred miles (321 km) per hour, with gusts so strong they could easily knock over a grown man. There was, however, positive news. Six crew members had stayed behind to search for him. Together, the seven men overwintered, and were rescued ten months later.

Bad luck happens and sometimes it happens a lot, but what Mawson has shown us is that we all have hidden strengths— physical strength, mental strength, and a real inner toughness, especially once we make a decision: *Never give up. Never give in.*

And most importantly of all, Mawson has shown that when luck really does run out, we still have the ability to search for inspiration in those darkest moments—and succeed.

Where do *you* seek inspiration? How will you find hidden strength when you need it? In modern life, one may not find oneself

---

[1] "The Quitter" by Robert Service was first published in book form in his collection *Rhymes of a Rolling Stone* in 1912. Robert Service was a British-Canadian poet, 1874-1958.

down a deep crevasse in a physical sense, but there are plenty of situations that can create a mental or emotional crevasse that one needs to "climb" out of. What would you have done in Mawson's situation?

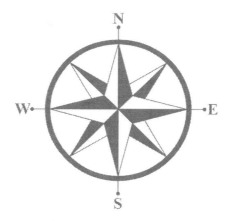

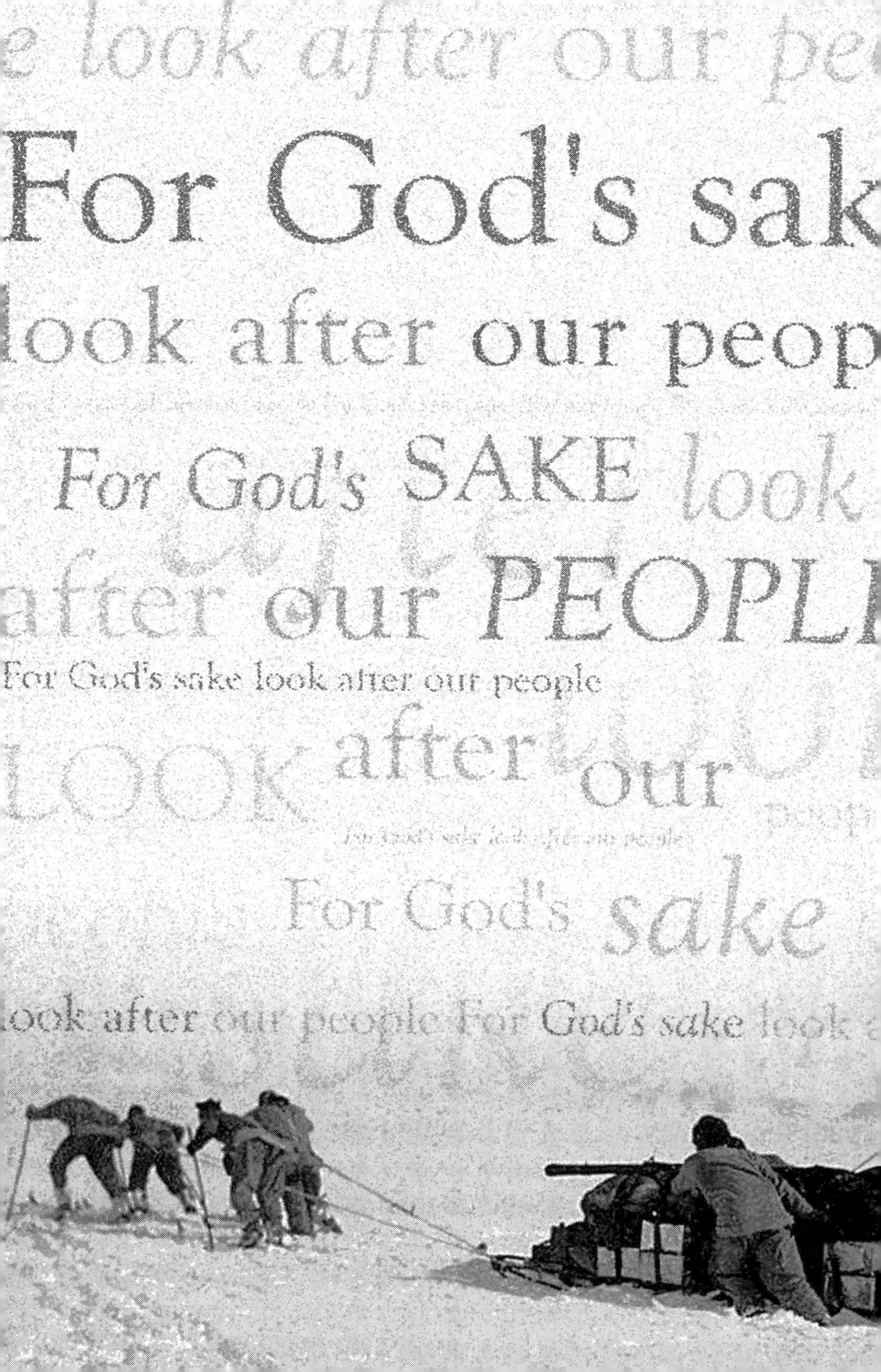
look after our pe
For God's sak
look after our peop
For God's SAKE look
after our PEOPL
For God's sake look after our people
LOOK after our
For God's sake
look after our people For God's sake look

What Do You Do When Luck Runs Out?

Crushing disappointments and the durability of the human spirit.

Luck. In every endeavor, there's luck. Good luck, bad luck—sometimes occurring at exactly the same time.

On the second expedition he led, Ernest Shackleton and his men were settled on a large floating ice slab in a temporary home they called Patience Camp. Over time that floe was whittled away to nothing, and the twenty-eight men took to the boats, heading for Elephant Island and camping each night on a nearby floe. Shackleton, sleepless early one morning, was pacing the floe when it suddenly split underneath one of the tents, plunging Ernest Holness, one of the men still in his sleeping bag, into the extremely cold water below. Shackleton reached into the water and pulled Holness and his sleeping bag to safety. In the next instant, the two halves of the floe smashed together with a thud, the solid ice crumbling to powder at the edges, and then just as quickly, parted again. Holness was saved, but he had to walk around for five hours to generate enough heat to dry out his clothing so it didn't freeze into one solid mass.

Was it *bad luck* that Holness was plunged into the icy water, or *good luck* that Shackleton was on hand to rescue him? The rescuer's reaction time had to be split second.

One way or another, luck just happens. It's present in every situation—work, relationships, when walking or driving or talking with people, and in all locations: at home, on holiday, in the office— and in virtually every field of interaction human beings will ever have. The best planning in the world can still be offset by external forces. We see it every day and in every newspaper: wrong person, wrong place, wrong time, or some combination of those factors.

Luck played a huge role in the heroic age of Antarctic exploration. Just as in the story of the split ice floe, there were instances of very good luck, and of bad luck so intense, it still burns indelibly into one's consciousness, even a hundred years after the event.

Bad luck happened in the heroic age of polar exploration, but something else happened there too. Arising from this bad luck came inspiring stories of how the men coped—how they battled the unexpected and faced the inevitable, conquering their fears and rising to the challenges.

Bad luck occurring in extreme climates is potentially lethal. What decision points, turning points and personality traits enabled them to face bad luck and not crumple under the pressure? What can we learn from them that can be applied when we face adversity in our own modern lives?

Luck has really and truly run out

Robert Scott's *Terra Nova* Expedition (1910-1913) had numerous goals building on the scientific, geological and meteorological assessments of Antarctica made during his earlier *Discovery* Expedition. The *Terra Nova* goals included new forays into previously unexplored parts of Antarctica, and being the first to reach the South Pole.

At the time Scott was planning his expedition, Roald Amundsen had not yet announced his plan to divert his Norwegian North Pole expedition southwards in a bid to conquer the South Pole first. (We discuss Amundsen's decision in the chapter entitled, *Do you agree all is fair in love, war and polar exploration?*)

Many of the scientific goals of Scott's *Terra Nova* Expedition were achieved. In addition, after a long and arduous struggle, Scott and four others—Edward Wilson, Birdie Bowers, Edgar Evans, and Lawrence "Titus" Oates—did reach the South Pole. Upon arriving at that barren, empty place, they discovered that their rival Amundsen had arrived there over a month before.

Imagine their disappointment—traveling 850 treacherous miles (1,368 km) on the frozen continent only to find that they had been beaten by a team that had come down for the sole purpose of racing them. It could have been seen as especially disheartening because Scott and his men had focused their efforts on the scientific purposes of their expedition in addition to reaching the Pole. Scott's journey had taken longer but was scientifically valuable. Amundsen's goal was just to win.

Amundsen left a tent at the South Pole. Inside were a few supplies and two letters. The first was for Scott, asking him to deliver the second to the King of Norway as proof that Amundsen had achieved priority. The famous photograph of Scott's five men from the *Terra Nova* Expedition at the South Pole gives a sense of both the strain the outward journey took on them, and the conditions of the day.

The return journey of Scott and his men was even tougher. Edgar Evans had cut his hand much earlier in the trip when they were adjusting the length of one of the sledges. The wound never healed, and he had severe frostbite. Even as the men struggled to survive, science was still a key goal. When the team stopped for a much-needed half-day break, Wilson, ever the keen scientist, found rocks and fossils of interest, thirty pounds of them (13.6kg), to be added to the sledge the men were pulling.

Evans died not long after, having suffered several head wounds during falls on the ice. Captain Oates struggled on, despite ailing and severely frostbitten feet and hands, but eventually, he too succumbed. Oates famously left the tent and never returned in an attempt to give the remaining three a fighting chance at survival.

Scott, Wilson and Bowers continued on, all in a weakened state. Extreme cold contributed to very poor surface conditions; the snow beneath the sledge runners had become more like sand, slowing down their progress despite Oates' heroic sacrifice. They went on short rations, and the lack of food further affected the men. Dwindling supplies of fuel oil reduced their ability to have the benefit from the warmth of a hot meal, and they all suffered from varying degrees of frostbite.

Before starting out from Cape Evans the previous November, Scott had left instructions for a dog sledge team to be sent out from their main base to meet them near One Ton Depot by a specific date, but for reasons that are still being debated today, that did not happen as planned. A prolonged blizzard trapped Scott, Wilson and Bowers in their tent for four more long, cold days.

Luck had really and truly run out—they died in their sleeping bags, in their tent, eleven miles (18 km) from One Ton Depot. The last entry in Scott's diary was March 29, 1912.

A search party discovered the tent six months later.

Their diaries and last letters to loved ones and expedition sponsors continue to inspire readers even today. They demonstrate a nobleness of purpose and achievement, of teamwork and camaraderie, of scientific endeavor, and a caring for the families they left behind.

Modern-day explorers, with all the advantages of the latest survival and communications equipment, and full knowledge of nutrition, say that after a hard day's travel in Antarctica they are so bone weary they can barely pick up a pencil. Yet, from Scott and his small team at the end of their days came some of the most memorable statements and writings in the English language.

"I am just going outside and may be some time."—Oates' immortal words right before leaving the tent for the last time.

Some of Scott's last words:

"Had we lived, I should have had a tale to tell of the hardihood, endurance, and courage of my companions which would have stirred the heart of every Englishman."

"For God's sake look after our people."

While lying in the tent dying, Scott wrote to Birdie Bowers' mother:

> "I write when we are very near the end of our journey, and I am finishing it in company with two gallant, noble gentlemen. One of these is your son. He has come to be one of my closest and soundest friends, and I appreciate his wonderful upright nature, his ability and energy.
>
> As the troubles have thickened his dauntless spirit ever shone brighter, and he has remained cheerful, hopeful and indomitable to the end."

In modern life we have many ways to face luck running out. The easy ones—giving up, blaming others, cursing the gods—seem never to have occurred to these early Antarctic explorers. They showed us a spirit, a purposefulness, and even a nobility in facing what life threw at them. Despite setback after setback, these men of the heroic age kept their humanity intact.

How do *you* face adversity?

A crushing disappointment

In 1914 Shackleton still had Antarctic ambitions. The Antarctic had held Shackleton under its spell since his "furthest south" journey with Scott and Wilson on the *Discovery* Expedition years earlier (1901-1904). His own subsequent *Nimrod* Expedition (officially called the British Antarctic Expedition, 1907-1909) got even closer, within one hundred geographical miles (185 km) of the South Pole.

The 1912 announcement of Roald Amundsen's success in being first to the Pole led Shackleton to concoct a bold, new scheme—to be the first to walk *across* continental Antarctica by way of the South Pole.

The plan would require two ships. One, the *Endurance*, would carry Shackleton, and the small group of men who would traverse the continent with him, to the Weddell Sea side of Antarctica. A second ship, the *Aurora*, would take another party led by Aeneas Mackintosh to the Ross Sea side. Starting from the previous expedition huts already there, Mackintosh and his men would lay depots along the Barrier toward the South Pole, so Shackleton and his men could pick up food and supplies once they had passed the South Pole and were homeward bound (the map on page 8 illustrates their plan).

Bad luck came in a number of ways to both parties. Since they had no means of communicating with each other, both parties had to confront head-on the situations they faced without help from the other ship. For this part of the story, we will focus on Shackleton and the *Endurance*. The fates of Mackintosh, his men, and the *Aurora* are equally compelling stories with highly memorable lessons about decision making in extreme environments, but we will save that for a later chapter called, *Promises, promises: How good are you at keeping yours?*

On the way south to the Antarctic, the *Endurance* anchored off the whaling port of Grytviken on the sub-Antarctic island of South Georgia. The whalers there warned Shackleton of the early onset of thick ice in the Weddell Sea, but after so much planning—and with World War I already raging—he didn't want to delay another year.

The *Endurance* set sail from South Georgia in December 1914. After an unlucky decision by Shackleton to pass by a possible landing site, rejected because it would have added many additional miles to the men's journey across the continent, the ship continued further south into the Weddell Sea. There she encountered thicker, more intense pack ice. On January 19, 1915, the *Endurance* became trapped in the ice, unable to retreat northeast to the first potential landing site, and unable to move forward to find another one.

By the end of February, it became clear that the ship would remain in place at the mercy of the ice through the Antarctic winter, from April at least until September. With good luck, by spring, the ice would break up and they would be able to navigate their way out. However, such luck was not with them. The shifting winter ice slowly crushed the ship, and by October the ship was irreparably damaged and would never sail again.

Imagine yourself in Shackleton's place. You watch the

heartbreaking slow drift of your ship toward the north with the movement of the pack ice. The *Endurance* is being crushed, and with it the dreams of your expedition southward. You are haunted by the spectre of financial ruin—without an expedition story to tell, there will be no way to raise money to pay back creditors. You hope beyond hope that the ship, which represents home for you and your men, will somehow survive—but you know deep down that it won't.

You also know that Mackintosh and his party on the Ross Sea side of the continent will take terrible risks to lay their depots in vain, and that you and the men you are responsible for may slowly die in this polar region, never having reached your goal. These same men are looking to you for inspiration, but each one knows there is no way out. In all likelihood, you are all doomed to a cold and painful death by exposure, madness, and starvation.

The ship was, indeed, crushed by the ice; all the men, tons of supplies, and three lifeboats were landed on the floating ice, safe there for a while. The wreck of the *Endurance*, held up by the ice, remained a constant reminder of all that had failed. Frank Hurley, the expedition photographer, was taking motion pictures of the wreck, half-submerged, at the *exact* moment the main mast snapped. This moving image captures that moment when their luck really *did* run out. Watching that flickering image more than a hundred years after the event evokes sadness, as one imagines what they all must have been thinking, standing on the ice, hearing the sickening crunch of the wood, watching the stout mast break in two like matchwood.

A new goal

Shackleton was an astute leader. He understood that his men were deeply discouraged at a time when they would need all their strength to survive. He had to give them a new purpose. If he couldn't achieve his goal of being the first to traverse the continent, what could he achieve? He re-framed his goal, his men's goals, and the expedition's goal into a single focus: to use all the means at their disposal to get home alive.

They were now camped on the ice, adrift on a large ice floe, nowhere near open water. The nearest known land was a few uninhabited islands, cold and forbidding, hundreds of miles away. The boats proved too heavy to drag across the ice for such a long distance. The men would have to wait out the northward drift until the ice broke up beneath them, then take to the boats and head for one of the uninhabited islands.

From that point, the nearest *inhabited* land that was practicable to reach given winds and current, was still eight hundred miles (1,300 km) away in South Georgia where they had started. Getting there would involve traveling across the world's roughest seas with waves up to fifty feet high. And the biggest lifeboat was only twenty-two-and-a-half-feet long.

The story of what happened to Shackleton and his men, and the decision lessons derived from their experiences, are covered in Chapters 6 and 10. However, the turning point, at the time that the *Endurance* broke up, was Shackleton instilling in his men the belief that if they worked together they could actually achieve the seemingly impossible.

Lessons for a modern age

Shackleton, Scott, Amundsen and Mawson stories run throughout this book. They truly made heroic decisions in the face of real adversity. They set goals. They took risks. And when faced with extreme adversity, they all found ways to endure, to achieve a measure of success, each in his own way.

Leaders like Shackleton and Scott faced head-on the worst of their experiences with a noble spirit. Scott's and Oates' dying phrases are lessons in humanity still taught a hundred years later in schools across the United Kingdom. Shackleton's bad luck led to his greatest legacy.

The feeling that luck has run out is often more perception than reality. How do some find a strong survival instinct at both an individual and a team level? What happened to Shackleton's men after the *Endurance* was crushed? We will explore these in subsequent chapters.

When facing a run of adversity in your business or personal life, due to situations that seem out of your control, can you do what Shackleton did—re-frame your own approach to bad luck? After all, the next best outcome might even turn out better than your original goal. Scott, Wilson, Bowers and Oates taught us about keeping your higher purpose in mind, and from Mawson as described in Chapter 2 – looking for external inspiration to boost your physical and mental state. Though gleaned from over one hundred years ago, it is intriguing that all of these approaches could be enormously beneficial in modern life.

* * *

Shackleton, Scott, Amundsen and Mawson all distinguished themselves in the field when the expeditions were underway, but their exceptional pre-expedition planning can sometimes be overlooked. Can you imagine how challenging it would be, in the age before computers and instant communication, to plan a multi-year expedition to a region that has no natural resources? It all comes down to knowing your needs before they arise. Not an easy task in any era—especially when your life may depend on it.

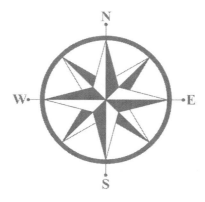

How Well Have You Prepared?

The art of knowing your needs before they arise.

I t's hard to imagine that one of the smallest, lightest objects imaginable—an ordinary match—could spell the difference between life and death, or success and failure, on a multi-year Antarctic expedition. But even small items like matches require planning. How many matches will be needed? How will they be kept dry enough to strike when a flame is a desperate need, without which the men of a field party may be doomed? Will the matches even strike, in the bitterest of cold?

What about the medicine chest—will medicines maintain full potency in their vials, once subjected to the extreme low temperatures? Opinions varied greatly in the early 1900s. What about snow goggles, navigational instruments, and flags to identify depots left on the ice—how many and what style? How much of anything is too much, how many are too many, and how many are not enough?

In the planning stages, all is speculation. The biggest challenge of all is that those needs that were not anticipated must be fulfilled in the field as they arise. But how do you do this in a land devoid of natural resources?

The art of knowing your needs before they arise

Preparation is the key to success. This thought holds true for any endeavor great or small, simple or complex. The compilation of a modern grocery list is not so different from that of equipping an Antarctic expedition—you have to anticipate all the needs that may arise before the next time you can get to the store. The difference between the two is largely in orders of magnitude—many orders of magnitude.

In filling a grocery list, with a store nearby, one can make good on whatever needs may have been overlooked with another trip to the store. Business planning can be more involved, because it looks much farther into the future. But there is a capacity to fill unanticipated needs as they arise, with resources readily devised or obtained. Antarctic expeditions are different in scope, fulfilment and risk. Every need for thirty or more men to survive in an alien environment for at least a full year, must be thought out to every conceivable end.

To achieve this, the planning must begin years in advance. Once the expedition has left a civilized harbor area in the Southern Hemisphere and is en route to the Antarctic, there will be no quick trip to the corner store, no easy resupply or rescue. The expedition's base will be far from shipping lanes; the nearest ports are thousands of miles away. Not only must the advance planning answer every single need for the entire time the expedition is away, it must also include elaborate backup plans in case the original has not performed to expectations.

All of this has to be achieved within a limited budget. The whole enterprise will have been financed by donations and credit before departure. There will be no cash to pay for anything but the most important requirements, with the hope that the balance of funds will come to hand when needed. It must all be fully repaid when the expedition returns with a positive outcome that can be presented in lecture tours, books, and photographic exhibitions.

The leaders of all of the heroic age expeditions faced these same challenges. Each had to simultaneously raise funds, obtain a ship, and find crews to man the ships and shore stations. They also needed to purchase a complete supply of ample food, fuel (including small, yet vital items like matches), shelter, and transport for the men who remained at the base and those who would explore further into the continent. Many of these decisions, made long in advance, could have life and death consequences later. These are just a few examples of the myriad of decisions—great and small—and some of them crucial—that needed to be addressed.

There were thousands of other questions, unanswered because they had yet to be asked. *How cold is cold?* Edward Wilson and his two companions were woefully unprepared for the -77°F (-60.5°C) temperatures they encountered on their Winter Journey in 1911. *How will you get drinking water from all this ice?* Putting snow into one's mouth to melt it results in little water, and dangerously lowers one's body temperature. Fuel for cooking and melting snow is vitally important, yet Scott found to his dismay that fuel loss occurred during months of storage in depots on the ice, most likely due to the cold conditions affecting the solder joints or the metal screw tops which used leather washers. *How many ponies and dogs will be needed? How much feed should you bring for them? How many motor sledges (and their spare parts) are too many, or too few?* All this had to be decided beforehand, when the expedition was still a glint in the leader's eye.

Planning in the days of limited communication

In the twenty-first century, we are accustomed to instantaneous communication, enabling easy adaptation to changing circumstances. All parties to a plan can know at the same moment when something has been changed, and what needs to be done. Perhaps someone wants to add another food item to a grocery list, or make a change in the route home to accomplish another errand. In business, a change in strategy can be shared and discussed by all the principals in a conference call. The plans evolve as needed, in real time.

In 1900, when Robert Scott was planning the first of the major British expeditions of the heroic era (the *Discovery* Expedition), the cable telegraph was the most advanced form of communication; wireless communication had yet to be perfected. Ships at sea had no way of knowing what had transpired ashore during the weeks- or months-long voyages. A change of plan made en route would not be known until the ship had come to port. In the case of the early explorers, selected sites were sometimes chosen as the location for a message post where notes could be left with the expectation of being found by scheduled relief ships.

At the time of the departure of Scott's *Discovery* Expedition, three locations that had been charted originally by James Clark Ross in 1840 were identified as Antarctic message posts. The *Discovery* erected red painted posts with brass cylinders at these locations: one at Cape Adare, one at Coulman Island, and the last at Cape Crozier. Visible from the sea, these posts contained detailed information as to the expedition's intentions for the next fields of exploration, or the selection of a wintering site.

The four essentials

In 1900, the field of polar exploration was not entirely new. Seafarers had been venturing north into the Arctic ice for centuries. The search for a Northwest Passage above the Americas had captured people's imagination since the sixteenth century. During Victorian times, this desire stimulated Britain's Royal Navy to send ship after ship into its icy clutches, to return—if they did at all—having failed in their mission.

In the 1890s Norway's Fridtjof Nansen had taken a different tack. He commissioned a ship to be designed to survive in the clutches of the ice pack, and using it, he came home with new knowledge about the sea ice and weather conditions of the far north. The consummate planner, he invented what he needed when it did not already exist—a ship that could not be crushed by the ice, as well as adapting the Primus stove and designing the Nansen cooker, both of which became essential equipment on all subsequent polar expeditions.

Robert Scott sought him out when setting up the *Discovery* Expedition since his aim was to unlock the secrets of the Antarctic. Scott spent months planning the mission, assembling the gear, and gathering the scientists and men of the crew who would bring home the successes in science and geographical observation. Other expeditions would follow in his wake, building on those successes. In the following few years, Shackleton, Scott himself, and the Australian Douglas Mawson would carry the flags of the British Empire further into the depths of the Southern Continent. Amundsen (from Norway), as well as others like Charcot (from France), Drygalski (from Germany), Nordenskjöld (Sweden) and Shirase (from Japan), would carry the flags of their own countries, all for the furtherance of geographical and scientific discovery along with their own national pride.

Regardless of which country they hailed from or what their overall aims were, these expeditions would all need the same essential equipment, and in planning their expeditions, an answer to these four overarching questions:

1. What is it we want to achieve?

2. Where is it we want to explore, and how do we plan to get there?

3. What will we need when we arrive, and for how long?

4. How is it all to be paid for?

Determine your goals before you start planning

One of most important things necessary for success was to have a clearly defined set of expedition goals. They needed a reason to explore the Antarctic: to fill in the empty spaces of the unknown world, to gather data for science's ever-growing demands, and to fulfil the personal goals of its leader whose vision aspired to something beyond an ordinary scope of work.

Why, after all, devote so much time and energy to getting a small number of human beings to a remote place that previous experience had shown to be no more than a navigational point on a featureless, colorless, empty, windswept, frozen plain? There was nothing to carry home from the place but themselves and a notebook full of meteorological data that no one else could bring. Why was it so important to men like Mawson, Shackleton, Scott and Amundsen to have this abstract goal of planting the flag of their respective nations in this ice?

It was an abstract goal in all these cases, yes. But it was a goal that lured all these men, the leaders and their followers to the utmost measures of devotion to duty, regardless of the outcome. Goals were also critical to fundraising, which had a direct impact on the important decision on what type of ship to take.

Getting there alive: finding a ship capable of surviving storms, ice, and overloading

The execution of these simply-stated goals was certainly not simple. All of the expeditions faced the challenge of finding the right ship with which to reach the Antarctic shores. The best building material for these ice-breaking ships was wood. It was flexible enough to bend without breaking under the extreme pressure of the moving pack ice that was certain to be encountered. A steel ship could be gored, and sunk.

The Dundee whalers of the 1890s provided a good model. Decades of experience in Baffin Bay off the coast of Greenland had shown the way: sailing vessels equipped with auxiliary steam power and constructed with good stout frames and planking. Sail power was essential since that reduced reliance on continually using the steam engine. There was no room for many tons of extra coal to drive the steam engine, when the holds were filled to overflowing with the supplies necessary to sustain a shore party for a full year or more. Scott's first expedition ship, the *Discovery,* was designed along these proven lines, and launched in 1901 for the express purpose of Antarctic exploration. She filled that role for later expeditions as well; when not exploring, she was engaged by the Hudson's Bay Company for its Arctic commerce. One of the two surviving expedition ships of the heroic age, she is now a museum ship, permanently positioned afloat at Discovery Point in Dundee, Scotland.

Like every Antarctic vessel ever launched, she had her limitations: slow, a heavy roller, and profligate of fuel. Shackleton, for his 1907 shot at the Pole, took another Dundee whaler, the diminutive *Nimrod*. For his next and final expedition in 1910, Scott chose the venerable steam whaler the *Terra Nova*. Later, Mawson purchased a Scots barquentine, the *Aurora*, which subsequently found another role in landing Shackleton's Ross Sea Party in 1915. These older vessels, purchased at a discount, survived to continue later in commercial trades.

Amundsen's *Fram* was Nansen's former Arctic ship, which was cleverly designed to survive the crushing grip of the ice pack. She had a hull structure enabling the ship to rise if the ice pressure squeezed her too hard. Her new diesel engine needed comparatively little fuel; her schooner sails gave slow but steady progress on Amundsen's long nonstop passage from Bundefjord, Norway to the Bay of Whales in Antarctica. It is the other surviving Antarctic expedition ship and is housed today in the *Fram* Museum in Oslo, the "Home of the world's strongest polar vessel."

In hindsight, Shackleton's decision to purchase the *Endurance* for his Imperial Trans-Antarctic Expedition in 1914 was unlucky. This ship was new but not designed specifically for exploration work. She had likewise been built to lift in the ice, but her hull—more for the comfort of the hunters for whom she had been designed—was not as rounded as that of the *Fram*. When the floes of the Weddell Sea closed around her, she did lift—but unfortunately not every time. She sank on November 21, 1915, a victim to the marauding ice.

These choices were largely the result of what was available when each expedition was in the planning stages, and the percentage of the overall budget that was devoted to the purchase of a ship.

The ship—purpose-built and new, or borrowed, or bought from secondhand stock at a bargain price—was invariably the largest single expense, and only after it had been met could attention be paid to the other, equally critical aspects of the enterprise.

Vital needs: a hut, sledging supplies, food for the men for one or more years

A failure in long-range planning for even one of these vital elements could, and did, have life and death consequences for the men involved in these expeditions. The needs for housing, at least, were relatively simple to prepare for.

How many men? The wintering parties varied in number from Scott's forty-six who lived in the icebound *Discovery* at Hut Point and just built a shore-based hut for their scientists to use, to Amundsen's nine at his base named Framheim, built on the potentially unstable Barrier Ice at the Bay of Whales. The huts themselves were simple wooden affairs, designed along the lines of settlers' houses, with numbered parts for easy assembly on shore. The space between their double walls and ceilings was filled with cork insulation to shield against the cold. Inside, coal stoves supplied the cook's requirements and kept the air temperature at a balmy 50°F (10°C). The fires were kept alight day and night from the tons of coal stacked in sacks outside.

Over the course of an Antarctic winter, the expedition leaders knew that the men's minds must be occupied. Lessons from earlier polar work revealed that some men could not take the prolonged darkness and extreme cold that kept everyone indoors for months at a time. Routine and regular work was required as well as providing a library for those of an enquiring mind: lectures and entertainment with a gramophone, games and even slide shows to be enjoyed in the evenings. The *Nimrod* Expedition brought a printing press and during the long winter months the men wrote and produced a book they titled *Aurora Australis*. The covers were made from wooden boards from packing crates. Somewhere between eighty and one hundred copies were printed in Antarctica and they are now highly treasured by museums and collectors.

The dogs and ponies brought for hauling sledges had an equally important value as the companions and warm-blooded wards of the men, who adopted them as pets. Every ship had its working cat; some of them came ashore. Amundsen provided a quintessentially Norwegian luxury: a sauna.

Food, glorious food

Even on ordinary working days in the hut, there was as much food as a man cared to eat. Once out on the trail, the fare was simpler. One-pot hooshes were the standard fare for breakfast, lunch and dinner. Dried milk plasmon and pemmican blocks of powdered meat were added to melted snow thickened with broken ship's biscuits, and taken hot the moment the mixture came to a boil. Hot tea or cocoa finished off the meal. The cooking pot and pannikins were scraped clean of every last morsel, the men had a smoke and prepared to move on. The sledges were laden with enough to supply the teams with what was assumed to be plenty to supply for their needs during the course of months that the longest journeys would entail.

How to feed the men? Again, a simple enough computation could determine the number of meals to be served over the anticipated duration of time ashore. All of it but the fresh meat of seals and penguins hunted on the spot would be in some way dried or canned in the relatively unsophisticated means of preservation of the day. This diet was enlivened on frequent occasions with special compositions from the galley, in copious abundance. The standard glory of the European tradition of Christmas was celebrated instead in June, with midwinter feasts hailing the approach of daylight after the darkest and longest of nights. In all of the expeditions the menu for these was as elaborate as the larder would bear, with toasts all around from the carefully rationed stock of alcohol.

Not all the food was held to be glorious. The locally hunted penguin meat had been aptly described as a combination of "beef, odiferous cod fish, and a canvas-backed duck roasted together in a pot, with blood and cod-liver oil for sauce."[2] Not the first choice of any of the men, but when times were rough and food very short, even this revolting combination would allay the pangs of hunger. After the crushing of Shackleton's *Endurance*, it led to their ultimate survival. Scott and Shackleton both intended to use the meat from their ponies, and Amundsen that of his dogs, slaughtered along their way to the Pole. Tough and stringy, it was barely edible, but served to give a little more nutritional value to the hoosh and was enjoyed by the surviving dogs.

The food quantities at least were anticipated and planned for in advance. But the food value of these meals, generous though it seemed to be at more than 4,600 calories per day, was not enough to supply the needs of overworked teams who were man-hauling at high altitudes. As Scott's and Shackleton's overland parties discovered, ever-increasing hunger became a scourge that could not be ignored. Those simple meals, coming at lunch and supper, were often the only bright spots in a brutally hard day. Only then would the hunger pangs be erased, and only for a little while.

Nutritional science was in its infancy in 1900. The word "vitamin" had yet to come into existence. The daily caloric requirements for hard work could only be guessed at. Even though every expedition had at least one physician on the team to treat injuries and frostbite as they occurred, none of those doctors really understood the causes of scurvy, or how best to treat it. While the beneficial effects of fresh vegetables and some fresh meats were well known, the vital component of vitamin C contained in them was not. They only knew that when the men were near shore, and eating the meat of the seals and penguins that were available there, their health was maintained. However, when the field parties were away for extended periods, scurvy was the result.

The disease had been a concern for centuries. On long sea voyages the men would bruise, then weaken as their muscles

---

[2] Dr. Frederick Cook's remark based on his experience on the *Belgica* Expedition 1897-1899.

became detached within their bodies, suffering joint pain, tooth loss, and eventually death. If they survived, their recovery was often remarkable, the result of the invisible vitamin C in various items of fresh food that became available once they had returned to shore. Seals abounded near the shore; their meat, eaten fresh, provided just enough ascorbic acid to keep the disease at bay. No one knew that drying the meat over heat reduced that value.

Other shortcomings appeared when the field parties, in an ill-considered attempt to increase the number of days they might advance toward their goal, decided to "spin-out" the ration by decreasing the total amount taken in a day. This had the dual effect of weakening the men, and aggravating their hunger to an intolerable degree. Rather than limit the number of days' advance, Shackleton and the men of his 1908 South Pole attempt continued well beyond the limits of their ration allotment. Their return to Cape Royds, which was a race against time and starvation, is described in Chapter 10, *Will The Results Be Worth The Effort?* They made it back by the barest of margins, mere hours before their ship, the *Nimrod*, departed for civilization for the winter.

Sledging supplies: the real work of the expedition

The leaders, in planning the expedition, knew that with the arrival of the Antarctic spring the real work of the expedition would begin. A separate list of supplies and materials must now be filled. Nansen's Primus stoves and annular cooking pots were vital equipment on all expeditions. Canvas tents, capable of being erected in high winds and able to sustain blizzard conditions were designed first to house three men, and later designs could house four or five men. Scott's three-man sleeping bags used in the *Discovery* Expedition gave way to the more comfortable, if colder, one-man bags. Preserved food of high caloric content was needed as well as windproof clothing, helmets, gloves and finneskoes—the list was endless, and the quantities a matter of speculation. Big and small details could not be neglected. Should they bring fur clothing, or wool and gabardine? Opinions differed on which was better. Every detail had to be thought out from the relative comfort of an office back home, months or years before the expedition would depart.

There were additional issues that could not have been anticipated until actual exploration was underway. Sledging equipment evolved over time. Scott believed in 1901 that sledges would glide better with German silver under-runners, but experience in the field showed that this was not always the case.

It was not until Wilson, Bowers and Cherry-Garrard's Winter Journey on the *Terra Nova* Expedition in 1911 that the special demands of *extreme* cold-weather sledging became known. In the very deep cold of winter, sleeping bags absorbed the moisture of sweat and breath, holding it there as ice, accumulating each night in ever greater weight. Clothing instantly froze into plates that felt like solid armor around the men when they rose each morning. They had to instantly stand in a man-hauling position or risk having their clothing frozen in an awkward position all day. The snow was so cold it could not melt under the friction of the sledge runners and give the necessary "glide." This last factor also played a major role in Scott's inevitable decline on the homeward journey from the Pole in 1912, when the weakened men found the snow beneath the sledges to be like sand under the runners.

Dogs, ponies, motor sledges or man-hauling: a cold, hard decision

Each leader had his own ideas as to the transport to be used in the field. In 1900, Scott was a product of his hierarchical Royal Navy experience. Throughout the search for the Northwest Passage, long-distance man-hauling had yielded impressive results; Scott found no particular need to enlist the help of other means. He did bring twenty-three dogs on the *Discovery* Expedition, but ironically, nobody skilled in their handling. As a result, the success of the dogs as transport was minimal for long journeys, though they did perform well on short journeys. Their health was impacted by being fed dried fish. They all died before their benefit could be fully realized, and man-hauling became their default sledge transport method.

In 1907, Shackleton realized he needed something better. Taking a cue from the Jackson-Harmsworth expedition to the Arctic in 1894-1897, he brought Siberian ponies to the Antarctic to move his supplies south toward the Pole. Despite the fact that they were woefully unsuited for the work, his ponies performed admirably—advancing the necessary supplies as far south as the Beardmore Glacier. Shackleton's success with ponies convinced Scott to take them as well in 1910 on the *Terra Nova* Expedition for his own advance on the South Pole.

Scott's detailed calculations (derived from previous British experience) seemed to prove Shackleton's idea about ponies right, but he was not dependent on ponies alone. For the *Terra Nova* Expedition, he also sailed with three specially adapted motor sledges and thirty dogs—all of which would help to move supplies. If all else failed, he would be satisfied to fall back on "good old British man-hauling."

Scott's careful planning seemed to have covered all the contingencies, but did not anticipate the challenges associated with the motor sledges and the early loss of many of the ponies. The remaining animals did their work well, but slowed the pace of the Barrier phase of the journey to the South Pole. There were too few dogs to move tons of supplies quickly. Most significantly, Scott did not anticipate the extent to which the physically gruelling man-hauling would run them down to the point where they could no longer walk. The photo on the cover of this book provides some idea of how challenging this was.

Amundsen was also a meticulous planner. His tactics, based on his previous experience in the Arctic, led him to a different decision. Rather than try modern methods like motor sledges, his study of Arctic native populations showed that well-trained sledge dogs in the hands of skilful and experienced dog sledge drivers could move heavy loads long distances over the snow and ice. They could transport him and a few explorers to the Pole and back. He knew that ponies, being herbivores, were not really suitable and motor transport for the ice was still experimental.

Amundsen was dependent on sledge dogs for his transport, but he had a detailed understanding of their needs, and brought with him many more than he would ultimately need. He set sail from Norway with ninety-seven dogs (arriving in Antarctica with 116 dogs, as some had had puppies along the way) and one of the best dog sledge drivers in the world, Sverre Hassel, to manage them. His decision proved to be successful, in that he was able to choose the fifty-five best dogs for his assault on the Pole in 1911.

From their research and experience, Amundsen and his team knew that among sledge dogs, there are natural leaders. But these lead dogs needed to know they were under the control of men, a relationship sometimes reinforced by the brutal lash. While Scott and Shackleton struggled with the few dogs they had brought, Amundsen's dogs, directed by their skilled human drivers, did their work with cool efficiency and got the expedition to the Pole and back with relative ease. They made it back to their base at Framheim while Scott's man-haulers were still coming down from the plateau. Amundsen proved that good planning, and being willing to learn from traditional sources, led to a highly successful outcome. Had Scott's luck with the motor sledges been better, a different assessment of their value might have resulted, and motorized Antarctic transport may have evolved more quickly in design and use.

By the time Douglas Mawson set out to investigate the two-thousand-mile wide swath of previously unexplored Antarctic coastline south of Australia, he had a wealth of recent data on which to base his choices for diet and transport. His losses were due to an accident and not the overextension of his human resources, and he returned with an impressive body of scientific and geographical results.

How is all this to be paid for?
Science and discovery as the sweetener

Exploration might represent freedom to an adventurer, but it was hardly free. Fundraising became the unenviable lot of every explorer, and the other side of each exploration's adventure. While governments were happy to advance their own prestige, they were not particularly generous at the first approach of an explorer with a plan. They would perhaps provide a little seed money, as a show of interest in expanding the reach of the realm, but it was up to the expedition to raise the rest. Public subscription helped, as did the backing of the geographical societies of the day if there were exciting prospects of discovery. But those in a position to contribute funds expected results, and often involved themselves in the setting of the goals.

Often the advancement of science was a potent sweetener to the plan. Meteorology was important to oceanic commerce. A deeper knowledge of the magnetic poles and global weather patterns could influence faster, safer passages for oceangoing ships. The related fields of gravitational studies and glaciology could yield similar benefits. The search for new land inevitably involved the search for new mineral resources to exploit for profit.

All these stoked the twin fires of curiosity and prestige, and fueled them further with the prospect of material gain. Even so, they were barely enough to get the ship out of the harbor.

All of the expedition leaders had to invest huge amounts of effort to raise the money needed to get the expedition underway. They faced enormous financial obligations and debts—personally guaranteed by the organizer—when expeditions were over and the ships had returned to port. The uncomfortable knowledge of this obligation haunted Scott, Shackleton and Amundsen.

Expect the unexpected: plan accordingly

Perhaps the greatest challenge in undertaking an expedition is: What do we do when things don't work according to the plan? What do we do when disaster strikes? Not every disaster can be predicted or averted. The more successful Antarctic expeditions were those with the greatest redundancy in supply, transport, and time allowance to address emergencies as they arose. Even the most astute advance planning had to have a backup plan, and the best had a backup for the backup.

Every polar expedition ran into situations that were not accounted for in the preliminary planning. Adversities of weather proved to be greater than could have been imagined. The sea ice in a given year did not behave as it had done in the past, and ships were prevented from reaching shore to pick up stranded parties, or offload crucial supplies. Unseen crevasses suddenly opened and swallowed dogs, sledges, and men, leaving those who survived with no easy means to trek to safety. Sudden frostbite, accident and injury, and the slow debilitation of scurvy weakened the once-hardy men who had so bravely set out on their journey. That so many survived even with these disasters is a tribute to the character of the men who journeyed alongside, or risked all to come in rescue.

Lessons learned

In modern life and business today, you are unlikely to be on an icy, snowy Antarctic coast getting ready to face a polar winter. There are, however, useful lessons from how early Antarctic expeditions were planned and provisioned that can be applied to one's own endeavors.

Key questions to ask yourself are:

- Have you studied in-depth the successes, failures and challenges your predecessors faced?

- Have you laid out your plans carefully, using that information?

- How good are you at anticipating every possible contingency and ensuring that all the materials are at hand to resolve them, when needed?

- What are the key elements you need to ensure survival and success, and do you have them in abundance? How will you improvise if you come up short?

And most importantly,

- If, once you have conducted your in-depth study of your predecessors, and you disagree with their method and strategy, are you confident enough to go against the accepted view and take a risk by following your own plan?

Even when every conceivable contingency has been accounted for during the planning of an enterprise great or small, it was often personal character and dedication to duty of the people involved, that led to the achievement of the goal. This raises another key question: Who have you chosen for *your* team?

As part of their planning, the early explorers had to choose officers, crew, experts, and advisors and transform them into high functioning teams. All of these decisions could—and did—have life or death consequences. This is the subject of our next two chapters.

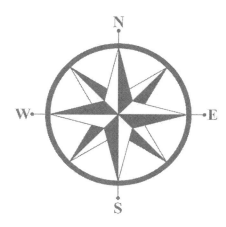

Who Is In Charge?

The surprising importance of the deputy leader.

In the heroic age of Antarctic exploration, teams were remarkably successful. A list of some of the many teams can be found in the *Tables* section on pages 178-183. Part of their success was due to selecting and motivating individual team members and giving them clear goals and appropriate levels of autonomy.

A key element was the expedition leader. Shackleton, Scott, Amundsen and Mawson all had characteristics of excellent leaders. They set goals, assembled first-rate teams, and each of their expeditions achieved a variety of successes, all in very challenging circumstances. One area that warrants more attention in both Antarctic literature and business management literature is how absolutely crucial the role of the deputy leader is.

The able lieutenant

In military parlance, "lieutenant" is a position of rank within the hierarchy of who gives the orders, and who follows them. The lieutenant in the navy, and the first mate on a merchant ship, answers to the captain, speaks to the men for him, and sees to it that his wishes are carried out. The position is one of secondary leadership, and it requires an intuitive grasp of when to follow orders, and when to give them, often on a moment's notice. In modern business parlance the captain is the CEO (chief executive officer) and the lieutenant is the COO (chief operating officer).

When the going gets tough—really tough—you want someone like Frank Wild on your team. Someone who, at the very start of the enterprise, when no one really knows any more than anyone else, steps into the breach and takes control of the situation. When the early-returning members of the first real foray of Scott's 1901 *Discovery* Expedition into the polar hinterlands met with disaster, one man kept his head. That man was Frank Wild.

An Able Seaman in the Royal Navy when selected for the *Discovery*, Wild had developed the resourcefulness and independence of thought that would serve him well in Antarctic expeditions yet to come. He was one of the twelve men who set off from the newly settled winter quarters on March 4, 1902 to update the relief mail post at Cape Crozier. Twelve days out, when it became obvious that the party must be split to allow some of the faltering men to return, nine of them turned for home under the leadership of Lt. Michael Barne.

A blizzard struck that party. Lost in the blinding drift, they became separated. Blundering onward in the hopes of better success, they were caught instead on a slippery slope of ice that ended with a drop into the sea. One by one they lost their footing and slid downward. One man, George Vince, went over the edge to his death. Frank Wild, a few feet above that dangerous, icy cliff edge, gathered the survivors around and led them back up to a safer location. Then he went onward through the still-raging blizzard, until he reached the ship and summoned help.

Had Wild not made that decision to immediately assume a leadership role, more men would have died. Possibly so many, that the success of Scott's first expedition would have been questioned, and the heroic age of polar exploration might never have occurred.

Wild had no more knowledge than anyone else of which way to turn, but he did have this: an enduring quality of self-composure and self-confidence that did not flinch in the face of disaster. This unique quality shone through again and again during the five expeditions in which he took part during the heroic age. With every one he grew in experience and stature.

Shackleton, when planning his 1907 assault on the South Pole on the *Nimrod* Expedition, wanted this man. On that expedition Wild was a key player, one of the three chosen by "the Boss" to man-haul with Shackleton up the Beardmore Glacier to within one hundred geographical miles (185 km) of the Pole. He had so proven himself as a valuable lieutenant, that in 1913 Mawson chose him to lead the six-man party that explored the limits of the western coast of Queen Mary Land. (Both stories are told in later chapters.) Having delivered notable results to that expedition, Wild was the obvious choice for the role of second-in-command of Shackleton's 1914 Imperial Trans-Antarctic Expedition, also known as the *Endurance* Expedition.

The true meaning of endurance

In Chapter 3, *What Do You Do When Luck Runs Out?* we described the events that led to Shackleton's abandonment of his goal to be the first to trek across continental Antarctica. We now continue the story because it perfectly illustrates the importance of an able lieutenant like Frank Wild being free to make decisions on his own.

As the *Endurance* was being crushed by the ice in the Weddell Sea, Shackleton and his men decamped to the ice. First they settled on an ice floe they called Ocean Camp and later transferred to another floe named Patience Camp. These floating ice pans were adrift in the pack ice and slowly moving northward, while at the same time breaking apart. The lack of safety and any visible way to travel for rescue played on some men's minds more than others. They had already been stuck on the ship in the ice for *ten months*, and now they were about to spend another *six months* camping on ice floes.

When the Patience Camp ice floe had drifted to the open sea and was on the verge of disintegrating in the slightly warmer water, they packed themselves into three small open-top lifeboats, the

Stancomb Wills, the *Dudley Docker,* and the *James Caird.* The men's diaries tell the full story of that six-day, incredibly dangerous boat journey. Weather was poor; the overloaded boats lay low in the water. The men were constantly wet, food was scarce, sleep was non-existent, and morale was at a low ebb. Some of the men began to succumb to exposure, and there was no way to restore their vitality. During the first day's travel the boats were in constant risk of being crushed by moving pieces of ice. The boats were of differing design and sailing ability; the challenge of keeping them all together added to the stress. Should either of the two smaller boats become separated from the others during the dark of night, the men in them were doomed.

Each boat was a team and the three teams had to work hard to stay connected. Some men rose to the challenge better than others. By the time they reached Elephant Island—a desolate, uninhabited rock *very* far from any whaling or shipping routes—some of the twenty-eight men were half-crazed from fear and exposure. One had suffered a mild heart attack, and Perce Blackborow's feet were so severely frostbitten, he could not stand on this welcome solid ground.

Rebuilding morale after a downturn is challenging in many organizations today. The challenge of rebuilding morale after experiencing more than four hundred days of isolation and still no source of rescue would be monumental.

The first point of landing was extremely hazardous, and no place to plan on staying. There was no visible source of food, and the watermarks on the rocks indicated the beach would be submerged at the highest tides. Frank Wild and a few of the stronger men immediately took one of the boats back out to sea and searched for several miles further along the coast to find a more hospitable site. Once identified, they returned, and the following day led all the men, boats and supplies safely ashore to this new location.

Good luck and bad luck attended the move, as it had the entire course of the expedition. The final camp was given the name Cape Wild—Cape Bloody Wild, some called it. The entire spit of land was covered in the most awful smelling guano, and the wind was so fierce at times it was hard to stand up. The good luck was that it was a secure landing area, above the reach of the highest tides, with easy access to seals and penguins for food. Seal blubber could be used as fuel for the stove.

Team survival

Shackleton knew that nothing rebuilds morale faster than hard teamwork to take everyone's mind off their still dire situation. He quickly concocted a plan to have McNish, the carpenter, strengthen the *James Caird*, the largest of the boats, and cover the deck, preparing it for another arduous voyage. Shackleton and five others would sail the *James Caird* eight hundred nautical miles (1,300 km), across the roughest seas in the world, to a whaling station on South Georgia. To keep the suspense, we'll save the story of that boat journey for a later chapter.

The intriguing part of the story from a team and leadership perspective concerns the question: how were the twenty-two men left behind on Elephant Island going to bind together and survive? Months of uncertainty lay ahead, even if the *James Caird* survived the journey and Shackleton was able to arrange for a rescue. It was far more likely that the twenty-two-and-a-half-foot boat and all her crew would be lost at sea, and the marooned men left to their own devices to survive and escape. They were left now with only the two smaller boats, neither of them at this stage suitable for any further ocean voyaging. Their only hope, if Shackleton did not survive, was to be found accidentally by a passing ship or to extract themselves in summer to a seasonal whaling station. Every man knew the possibility of this was extremely remote, and winter was coming on.

Team survival is based on many factors. One of these is belief in their leader. Shackleton, Wild, Crean, Hurley, and a few others proved their merit as leaders over and over during the four hundred days of entrapment on the ice. They proved it again on the previous six days on the risky boat journey to Elephant Island.

In Chapter 6 we ask the question *Who's On Your Team?* to get at the heart of team building. For the daring boat voyage from Elephant Island to South Georgia, Shackleton logically chose the very best sailors. He left no doubt among those staying behind that he had not compromised in choosing the very best men to make the voyage, and that he had every intention of winning through and bringing a relief ship as soon as he could.

He appointed Frank Wild in charge of the twenty-two men who must remain on Elephant Island to await their fates. Wild was well-liked by the men, and an accomplished polar explorer. Shackleton left written and verbal instructions on what to do if he did not make it back to rescue them. This included some forward-thinking details on arranging a sale of the expedition photographs which Hurley had previously retrieved by diving into the icy water of the slowly sinking *Endurance,* and who should write the expedition book and give fundraising lectures to pay back creditors.

"Lash up and stow"

As soon as the *James Caird* sailed out of sight, Frank Wild instituted a set of routines. He understood that structured time, leadership and belief that rescue might be possible would help to keep the men working as a team. They gathered together enough rocks to build two four-foot-high walls, nineteen feet apart—the foundation for a primitive hut with the two upturned boats for a roof, and sailcloth walls. There was to be no standing up in this hovel, and barely enough room to spread the sleeping bags. With no change of clothing, and the reeking guano beneath their bags, the situation would have strained anyone's temper. They had already been together for so long, one could easily imagine that every story had been told, and every song had been sung. Cliques, temperaments, and personality clashes would already have been long established.

Every morning, Wild would say, *"Lash up and stow; the Boss may come today."* It wasn't a simple wake-up call. It was an order to pack up their sleeping bags and kits, so their very small makeshift hut could be used as a seating area during the day. It was also a double-edged instruction implying that Shackleton—"the Boss"—would never let them down, and that they in turn should not let him down by being anything other than the brave, true men he would expect to find upon his return.

Wild's daily instructions also reinforced the idea that a routine was important for maintaining morale. More importantly, it reinforced the expedition hierarchy. Wild might be in charge on Elephant Island, but Shackleton was still the expedition leader, and ultimately they all answered to "the Boss."

On Elephant Island, meal times were fixed. There was a designated seating arrangement for each meal, enabling the men to shift around in a sequence so each day they each would have one meal when they were closest to the fire, and the other meals that day further away from the warmth. Afternoon time was allocated to catching penguins and other activities. Saturday nights were reserved for Hussey's banjo and topical songs that made fun of members of the team. If someone objected to what was sung about them, an even more critical song was composed for performance the following week.

Frank Wild also tried to reinforce the belief in their eventual rescue by reducing the amount of seals and penguins they stockpiled for the winter. This plan proved to be as controversial as it was inspiring as time slipped on from one month—to two months—to three months—and still no sign of Shackleton. However, the men stayed jelled as a team, intent on not letting "the Boss" down if and when he ever returned.

Structure, purpose, and belief

Survival depends on so many factors, both at an individual and team level. Those most capable of surviving are not always the ones who look physically strong. Mental toughness, coupled with a sense of purpose, can be a far more important ingredient.

That the men on Elephant Island did not descend into anarchy, madness or murder was due to leaders who instinctively understood how to keep them motivated in extreme conditions.

Frank Wild inspired them, but he did so much more. The best qualities of leadership are not something that can be taught. They must be grown into as a process of maturing through a wide variety of experience.

Wild was not a born leader. Small of stature and mild of manner, he did not seem destined for command. He started off his Antarctic career as a low ranking man on the *Discovery* in 1901, but showed then that when the circumstances demanded some measure of leadership, that he could step into the role without a second thought. He faced every extreme demand with the same cool detachment, as though it were something he did every day. Years later, when Mawson put him in charge of five men set on the shore fifteen hundred miles (2,400 km) from any other human beings, to chart and explore that shore, he rose to the task. Every expedition he ever took part in served to hone that capacity. Yet he never aspired to the overall leadership of an expedition. He knew the place he wanted—that of the best sort of lieutenant, to carry out the expectations of those who planned and executed the expeditions.

Wild was not the only man who proved himself able to step into the role of deputy leader when circumstances demanded it. Chapter 7 shows how Tom Crean and William Lashly stepped in and made the decisions when Lt. Evans was felled by scurvy. In Chapter 8 we see how Ernest Joyce, a man who never aspired to leadership, rose to the challenge far out on the Barrier when the nominal captain Aeneas Mackintosh could no longer lead the team.

When facing challenging decisions in business, there are many lessons that can be applied. Do you have a Frank Wild on your team? If so, have you given your able lieutenant free range to make the very best decisions in the moment, or is he or she hampered by complex or conflicting instructions?

When you are either in business or personal relationships involving a challenging team situation, can you do what Wild and

Shackleton did, and create structure, purpose, and belief?

In addition to having an able lieutenant, it is important to have the best team members possible. The next chapter explains how this was achieved. Some of the selection criteria might surprise you!

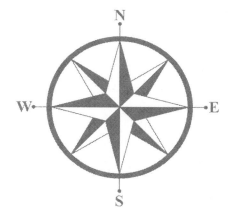

Who Is On Your Team?

Choosing the best from the best available.

T he question is apt in almost any endeavor, across any era in history, and in any place in the world. Who is on *your* team?

Ideally, every single person has been interviewed, vetted, and put through a meticulous process to identify just the right one for the position. This is certainly true of those who took part in the exploration of the Antarctic in the early days. Everyone—each biologist, geologist, meteorologist, explorer, doctor, photographer, cook, able-bodied seaman, and officer who found himself there for the first time had been specifically chosen for the job.

Most of the expedition leaders had hundreds of willing applicants to choose from, assessing each with due care and caution, and seeking the most qualified and most adaptable. This time-honored and generally successful approach works well in any business.

Under duress, however, some of these choices proved less than satisfactory in their leaders' eyes. Scott, after the first season's work in the *Discovery* Expedition, decided to take over the plateau exploration from Lt. Armitage, and to send Shackleton home after he had physically collapsed on the return of their southern journey. Amundsen had his bout with Fredrik Hjalmar Johansen—a famed

Norwegian explorer in his own right—and decided to leave him behind to survey the area east of the Framheim base, taking another in his place for the glory of being first to the Pole. Shackleton had to deal with a near mutiny on the ice initiated by one or two of the men after the *Endurance* sank.

When looking at all the expeditions, it becomes clear that some men rose to the challenge, and some were diminished by it. Are these the results of inadequate vetting from the comfort of a home or office, or of misinformation by applicants who may have overstated their qualifications? No doubt some of each, but by and large the leaders of these early expeditions—Scott, Shackleton, Amundsen and Mawson—were quite astute when it came to deciding who would be a part of their team.

Apocryphal stories abound of Shackleton's often whimsical and certainly spur-of-the-moment selections of who would accompany him into the frozen unknown. Wordie's spectacles attracted him, as did Hussey's banjo and the fact that he "looked funny." Yet, remarkably, Shackleton's quick assessments led to a diverse and skillful team. Scott took mostly Royal Navy men for the crew of the *Discovery*. They were already accustomed to the naval hierarchy and ready to follow orders without question. Seaman Tom Crean joined the expedition in New Zealand almost on a whim, when an opening presented itself which he volunteered to fill. Frank Wild had already proven himself on the long voyage the *Discovery* took from London to New Zealand en route to the Antarctic. The merchant sailors among the crew were less adaptable, and ready to return with the relief ship, the *Morning*, after their first winter-over.

Amundsen likewise chose his officers from the Norwegian Navy, who were already versed in ice navigation and ship-keeping in polar conditions. His carefully detailed plan called for a "quick" run to the Pole and back. To that end, he included a ski champion, Olav Bjaaland, and skilled dog drivers, Helmer Hanssen and Sverre Hassel, to manage the 116 dogs he would be landing on the ice. To fill the all-important role of cook for the ship and the Antarctic base camp, he brought along Adolf Lindstrøm, a veteran of his historic 1906 transit of the Northwest Passage.

Most of those who journeyed to the Antarctic in the early expeditions had yet to be wed, and seized upon the opportunity to enhance their academic or military standings, or pursue the science to which they were already betrothed. The *Discovery* carried some young scientists (such as Hartley Ferrar, a geologist) who were just beginning their careers. The same can be said of the young officers, who were moving up through the ranks while charting a strange new world for the armchair travelers at home. Even the seamen, with smaller chances of advancement through the ranks, gained at least a trove of adventures with which to regale their fellows in the mess deck.

Whatever their role, more than a few found themselves drawn to the place for a second, third, fourth, and even fifth time. Knowing its dangers and adversities after their first expedition, they had *chosen* to go back there, to this inhospitable place, to meet and conquer its challenges, together. For some, their presence became a validation of the Victorian poet Tennyson's call in *Ulysses*, to prove in these unequal trials, "one equal temper of heroic hearts."

Not every man was up to the task. Some found these trials to be too much, and the rewards too few. But those who were, and committed their physical and spiritual energy to the massive enterprise at hand, gave and received rewards not to be found at home.

The same is true in all walks of life. Beyond the obvious physical and educational requirements of a position, often unseen forces drive us; logic fails and aspiration fills the gap. Those with like-minded aspirations combine forces and risk it all in business, in love, in war, and in exploration. Who is to be on the team? Who *wants* to be? Who *will* be?

Hints to travelers

Every era has boundaries to its known world, and yields a place of honor to those who cross those boundaries to open up vistas once only imagined. And those who venture forth seldom go alone; the work is too great to be undertaken by a single person. Some of these men came back again and again, growing in maturity of years and polar experience. They became the senior members teaching the new recruits who were filling the ranks of the expeditions that followed.

The transmission of hard lessons from mentor to raw recruit allowed one expedition to build successfully on the results of those preceding it. There was a continuum of shared knowledge and experience across expeditions led by Scott and Shackleton, who were rivals in their quest for the Pole. This is nowhere more evident than in the *Discovery* Expedition's very first overnight foray out onto the Great Ice Barrier when six men set off man-hauling a sledge laden with one three-man tent and a cooker that no one knew how to light. Such misapprehension of life on the trail was slow to dissipate, but by the end of the ship's two-year stay at Hut Point, Scott was confident enough in their abilities to lead two men out over the featureless plateau, with limited navigational aids, and was certain that they would safely return.

Five weeks out from Hut Point and seven thousand feet up the Ferrar Glacier, he had arrived with his full supporting party of twelve to the edge of the plateau. A flat, featureless plain lay before them, slowly rising in the distance from their high camp just beyond the last nunataks (exposed ridges) marking the head of the glacier.

In an unfortunate accident, their copy of the book, *Hints to Travelers*, containing the necessary tables to compute longitude, had been blown away somewhere back along the trail. Without it there would be no sure way of finding their way back out of the plateau, to the exact spot where their highest depot of food and supplies would be waiting. Scott, ever resourceful, suggested an alternative—a penciled copy of data drawn from memory and written down on the spot. On this, his own life and the lives of the advance party would entirely depend. That two men would voluntarily risk their lives on such a flimsy record says much about their faith in their leader, and his faith in them. From that moment forward they were simply three men in a tent, equal to each other in every way but that of leadership.

They marched outward into the frozen desert for ten days, covering 160 miles (257 km) after the other nine men had turned for home. Cold, hard work and a shortage of rations were taking their toll, and fuel for the Primus stove was running low. Scott determined they had reached the end of their tether, and the time had come to turn for home. It was on that return that a snow bridge without notice broke away from beneath their footsteps and two of the three men suddenly disappeared into a yawning crevasse. William Lashly, caught off-guard on the surface, threw himself on the ground and hauled back with all his might on the sledge. Twelve feet down, Scott and Petty Officer Edgar "Taff" Evans (unrelated to Lt. Edward Evans whom you will meet in Chapter 7) dangled at the extremity of their harnesses, slowly spinning in the air between the blue-white ice walls of the crevasse, reassuring each other in matter-of-fact tones that they were, indeed, all right.

Above their heads, the broken sledge lay like a bridge across the mouth of the crevasse; the position was still gravely dangerous. And the moment Lashly relaxed his grip, the sledge slipped further. The two men dangling below would not last long in the cold there, nor would Lashly, who was striving with all his might to keep the sledge from dropping into the crevasse. There was no one within two hundred miles (320 km)—they would have to save themselves. Death for all three was only minutes away.

Scott, losing body heat quickly, knew he had to act fast. He swung himself at the end of his tether until he could get a foothold on a small ledge of ice, threw off his mitts and began pulling himself up, hand-over-hand toward the lip of the crevasse. Desperation drove him to the top, and he grappled his way over the lip with superhuman strength. Lashly, pushing back with all his might against the sledge, could only watch.

Scott did it, but his hands were frozen, white to the wrists. He warmed them for five minutes on his breast, and then turned to help Lashly at the sledge. In another minute Evans too was safe on top. For a few moments, the men could only look at each other. They wasted no time in patching up the sledge and moving onward, still using Scott's handwritten tables to guide them. By six o'clock that evening, they had reached the first of the depots left on the homeward trail. At that moment, there were no leaders here, and no followers, just three men on an equal footing—saved by the barest margin, thanks to quick thinking and reserves of strength hidden in each before this moment. They, too, were a remarkable team, carefully chosen for their skills and teamwork.

One of the most interesting aspects of the teams in the Antarctic at that time, was that most men instinctively knew when to follow their leader and when to act independently. But there was always an expectation that the men would be resourceful as a team when they needed to be. Had Scott been a different type of leader, or as found in some businesses today, a micro-manager, the outcome could have been very different.

Proven in the field

Petty Officer Taff Evans and Leading Stoker William Lashly were of the lower deck. Young men of twenty-four and twenty-six, they were seamen whose career paths in the Royal Navy were nearing their zeniths, with retirement pensions coming due many years in the future. They so impressed Scott with their unflappable durability and devotion to duty that he wanted them along on his next expedition, which was already germinating in his mind. When asked to join him again on the *Terra Nova* in 1910, both readily agreed.

These were two among many of the *Discovery* who returned to explore Antarctica. Of the seamen, Tom Williamson, Frank Wild, Ernest Joyce, and Tom Crean also came back, in one expedition or another. From the wardroom or officer ranks, there was Dr. Edward Wilson and Lt. Edward Evans of the *Morning,* and of course, Ernest Shackleton. Some of them came back and died here. Others came back once and then never again. And some, like Crean, Wild and Shackleton himself, could not seem to get enough of the place. This book is filled with their stories and their polar decisions.

The names of the leaders of these expeditions are of course the best known. That is as it should be. Without their energy, commitment and desire, expressed with wholehearted conviction from the very beginning, the expeditions themselves would never have left the safe shores of home. But while the familiar names belong to those who led, they would be nothing without the additional men who along with the leaders, shared in hauling gear, pitching camp, and walking the long treks, steadfast and enduring. Without them, there would be no leaders. There would be no survivors, and no story to be told.

On Followership

One of the key qualities of leadership is knowing the value of competent, dedicated followers who are prepared to step into positions of greater authority when needed. The role of "followership" demands its own set of strengths. During the heroic age, in addition to physical endurance and a well-learned set of survival skills, the most important traits included loyalty, pride of place, a powerful work ethic, honesty and team commitment.

This included a deep-rooted sense of duty and obligation to a larger cause, often illustrated by personal effort beyond what might have been expected. It included a sense of discretion, an intrinsic understanding of what must be said and done, and what must not.

It also included recognition of one's position in the hierarchy. Not everyone aspired to be a leader. Those who do not, who are happy with their level in the world and the value of the work they do, often go unrecognized. Some of their stories are revealed in this book. There are many more amazing stories that can be found in the diaries of the men who were not leaders.

Not a perfect art

There were, of course, some in every expedition who did not fit in well in either role. Their stories are important too, but less often told. In his *Discovery* Expedition, Scott found it expedient to send home several of the merchant seamen who had never quite got on in the mess deck with the Royal Navy sailors. In the tense days after the sinking of Shackleton's *Endurance*, Thomas Orde Lees was widely derided as lazy, and above menial work. He became the butt of jokes, the lowest man in the pecking order of the castaways. Somebody had to fill that role, for the greater cohesiveness of the rest. The carpenter Harry "Chippy" McNish had the temerity to challenge Shackleton with common sense on the ice, and never regained stature after his act of near-mutiny.

There were others who did not fare well—they were unsuited by temperament or physical stamina for the rigors of the polar winters. They withdrew from the society of their fellows into their private mental sequesters, unable to function well in the tasks for which they had initially been chosen. No one was to blame for this, but everyone had to be able to adapt to changing circumstances.

The ends of the Earth

To face the challenges of Antarctic exploration, effective teamwork required more than just a well-chosen core group of members. The leader had to be highly competent in his role. He needed a strong moral compass so his actions would inspire his men to follow him into the unknown and trust that he would bring them all home alive.

There are too many examples to name, but here are a few of the very best. Scott brought his two seamen back from the plateau in 1904. Shackleton brought his three men back from nearest the Pole in 1909. Wilson brought Bowers and Cherry-Garrard back from the winter trek to Cape Crozier in 1911, "the worst journey in the world." Amundsen led his team to the South Pole and made it seem like an easy walk. Victor Campbell brought back his five men after one of the hardest winters ever endured, surviving in an ice cave. Frank Wild was left in charge on Elephant Island, and kept the men safe until Shackleton's return in a relief ship.

Each of these men had a definite aura of self-confidence in his chosen role, which, even in the darkest nights, in the face of unimaginable travail and certain doom, inspired the men in their command. It may seem like a hyperbole to say that men would follow these leaders to the ends of the earth, but in fact, they *did*. Without such inspiration, in many cases the exploration party would have lost faith, weakened, and some or all would have perished.

Who is on your team?

If the members have been well chosen, everyone from the experienced leader at the top, down to the raw recruit with everything to learn, will pull together towards a common goal, working as a team and becoming stronger as a result. Shackleton was blessed to have had someone as hard-working, agile, and dedicated as Frank Wild, but his presence was the result of Shackleton's skill in choosing.

Take a moment to ask yourself: What teams are *you* on? Can you rely without question on your teammates? Do your collective skills complement one another? How good are *your* leaders? Most important of all, would you go with them to the ends of the Earth?

Who's on *your* team?

* * *

Seven men followed Robert Scott to the high plateau in an attempt to reach the South Pole first. Five headed onward for the Pole itself; three, serving as the support team to get Scott and his team to this point, turned about and headed for home. While still hundreds of miles from home, one of them became so ill from scurvy he could barely walk. Sometimes extreme demands are made on us, and we are forced to make decisions and take risks that seem impossible. In the Antarctic, life and death might hang in the balance, and the outcome might depend on one man to pull through against all odds, or all would face certain death.

One man had to, with only three biscuits, and thirty-five miles (56 km) of frozen terrain to cross. Would you have volunteered to do it?

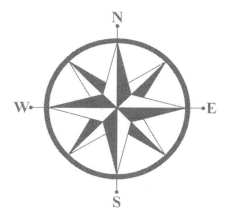

Three Biscuits And Thirty-five Miles To Go

Would you do it?

Think of a city 750 miles (1,200 km) from where you are right now. Imagine yourself walking there, cross-country in the dead of winter, pulling with you everything you will need along the way. "Everything" includes your tent and sleeping bag, all your food and the means to prepare it, the fuel to melt the ice for drinking water, heavy navigational instruments, and of course a sledge on which to haul it all.

The moment you arrive, you turn around and start walking all the way back to where you started.

Imagine that you have embarked upon this journey with seven others, and that during your two months together all of you became closer through this shared experience. Soon you will be parting company—some to continue on toward a still more distant goal, and some to return. The four who will go on are of course those most fit to do so; those sent home have not quite made the grade. Your leader will decide today who stays and who returns.

For those returning, there will be nothing new—no discovery, no glory—just a long and dreary walk until you reach base once more.

There is no desert in the world so bare as this, so empty and devoid of any scrap of life—not even a stone—to delight the eye or interest the mind. It goes on like this for hundreds and hundreds of miles, to the far side of the continent, without so much as the nunatak peak of a buried mountain to mark a way across. The coldest of winds sweeps the drifts of snow in every direction. There is no way out but the return of the way in, where the meagre depots are planted at the slimmest of margins, to guide and sustain the traveler home.

The Pole itself, 172 miles (277 km) farther on, is clearly in hand, and the time has come for the last supporting party to detach itself and return home. The question on your mind is will you be one of the team to go on to the Pole? Will you want to be?

The best-laid plans

January 3, 1912. Captain Robert Scott's assault on the South Pole has made good progress. His men have reached their goal on schedule, this parting-place on the South Polar Plateau. Eight men in two four-man teams have been working steadily since the beginning of November, 1911 to reach this place, first with the aid of ponies, and since December 9, man-hauling their gear over an eight-thousand-foot (2,414 meters) ascent up the Beardmore Glacier to this plateau.

Scott comes into the tent of the returning party and delivers a startling announcement: he will take one person from the four-man team and add him to the team who will be going forward with him to the South Pole. The new idea is that if four could make the final dash, then five can do it faster, so much so that they will catch up with the three-man support party just before they reach home base. The fourth man, Birdie Bowers, goes over to Scott's tent to join the Polar Party, leaving Tom Crean and Bill Lashly to turn homeward under the command of Lt. Edward Evans.

So, this is the way it would be—five men to go on, three to return. There was nothing for it but to trust Scott's wisdom, follow his orders, and believe that all would be for the best. After a long parley over things in general, Scott, confident of success, thanks them one and all for the generous way in which they have assisted in the final goal, and assures them that he will be sorry when they part.

The change from two four-man teams meant that much of the depot supplies would have to be recast into three- and five-man units, with no mistakes in the division. Scott asks the men of the supporting party if they will be all right making the 750-mile return trip as a party of three. "Of course," responds the leader of the party, Lt. Edward Evans. The two others, Tom Crean and Bill Lashly, mutely nod their assent.

Experience had shown that four-man teams worked best in man-hauling long distances, but in the 1900s, an order from a commanding officer had to be obeyed. Would you have dared to voice your opinion?

Facing difficulties as they arise

It was a day of cold drift, as cold as any they'd yet encountered. Even so, they all made one good last outward march together, twelve more miles (19 km) toward the Pole. There had to be a point, a place where no further help was needed, and each team must look to its own affairs. Here was the true farewell, the final goodbye. The fates of all who had struggled equally to gain this far advance would now fall out to different advantage. The empty plain surrounded them in their parting. A vast cathedral with no walls was now instead an airy vault that could not contain the awesome consequence of this moment. The last supporting party gave three cheers for their friends and said goodbye. Now, watching the others disappear into the white wilderness ahead, the supporting party turned in their tracks to take those first steps, dragging their sledge behind. Their own story was just beginning.

There were, perhaps, no three men lonelier in all the world. The remoteness of their advanced position was exceeded by only that of the five who were now on their way to glory and the Pole. But, in their suddenly diminished company, they felt their isolation yet more acutely. It drew them together, men and officer, encircled them, and seemed to ease the proper distinctions of rank and class.

The journey back to Hut Point and safety would be a long one—a minimum of forty-four days. That timing depended on perfect Antarctic weather and good snow conditions, both of which were unlikely, and achieving their desired seventeen miles (27 km) per day—a dreadfully extended haul under any circumstances. Coupled with the outward march to this godforsaken place, it would give them, for a brief moment, the distance record for the longest polar march ever done—fifteen hundred miles (2,400 km) for the roundtrip, give or take a few. It was not a record that brought much joy to contemplate. Before long it would be exceeded by that of the Polar Party, who would also expect to enjoy that other, dearer, record—that of having been the first men to stand on the South Pole of the Earth.

Taking up their load with a will, they made thirteen miles (21 km) before camping for their first night on the homeward trail. Here on the plateau, they had no landmarks of any kind to triangulate their progress. They would be dependent on sighting the outward-bound cairns they had built of blocks of snow set at predefined distances apart, to show them where they were. All of a sudden it seemed as though the unequal division of the company was a huge mistake, and the burden of it must be borne by these three men. No great matter; these things are what they are. Success comes from not dwelling on why they were in the situation, but on moving forward in their new circumstances as a team of three.

The eye searches in vain for some dark object, some shadow to break the white monotony of the trail ahead, but there is nothing. Snow goggles are well enough for the pullers, but the man leading the way needs better vision to pick out the indistinct humps of weathered snow-cairns in the distance. Up and on the road after breakfast, Crean led the way, his eyes fully exposed to the strong light above and reflecting off the snow. By early afternoon the telltale stinging told him it was too late to stop the damage. He wouldn't be sleeping much; zinc tablets from the medicine kit gave but scant relief. He'd march blind while the others took the lead.

They led him seventeen miles (27 km) that second homeward day, and another sixteen-and-a-half the next. Along the way they passed the remains of their old depot camp with four pairs of skis sticking up out of the snow—one pair for each of them, and one for Birdie to pick up on his way home. Evans kept them going at a pace, anxious to make the Upper Glacier Depot before their oil for cooking and melting snow into drinkable water ran out.

The descent became more difficult, and the sledge harder to control as the glacier beneath them inclined down into the upper reaches of the gorge. They had reached the head of the icefalls found by Shackleton on his own return from the plateau in 1909. This torrent of ice, fractured by deep blue crevasses crossing in every direction, descended abruptly into the upper reaches of the Beardmore Glacier. From the top, there was no way through to be seen; circling around the ice falls would add days to the journey risking further exposure and starvation. Coyly beckoning, the smooth traveling surface of the upper glacier lay in full view hundreds of feet below.

The party crept along, lost in a welter of dangers at every turn. They came at last to a brink over which they could not hope to control the sledge. If they were to go forward at all, it would be aboard, as passengers on a runaway, to whatever fate might deal them at the bottom of the slope. There would be no going back.

The men inched along toward the brink, grabbed on, and tipped themselves into the drop. The sledge ran down the slope, picking up speed beyond any sort of control. It must have reached sixty miles (96 km) per hour, and yet by some miracle kept upright and on course, bumping mightily over unseen obstacles, clattering uncontrollably over hummocks of hard ice. Without warning it left the ice altogether and leapt into the air, catapulting clear over the blue depths of a yawning crevasse. By a divine miracle of coincidence, the sledge was brought up to a hard standing by an old lunch camp near the Upper Glacier Depot they had used on the outward journey.

Given the choice of destruction by accident versus death by starvation and exposure, which would you have chosen?

Bridges to be crossed

Carefully dividing the rations in the depot and taking no more than their fair share of pemmican, biscuits, and oil, they moved on. Another hundred miles (160 km) down the glacier, and another four hundred (640 km) across the relatively easier flat barrier would see them home. Bright sunshine gave way to a low-lying cloud that filled the valley with a dense fog. The slope of the glacier drove their route far to the west where a pair of tributary glaciers flowed into the Beardmore Glacier at the same level, churning up a perfect nightmare of crevasses. These mazes are hard to see even in good light, and easy enough to work into. By the second day it was clear the party had slipped into a trap.

Great tumbled blocks of ice the size of churches loomed through the floating crystals. A tangled web of passages ran between them. Enormous chasms, deep enough to swallow whole the biggest ship afloat, appeared abruptly.

The three men came to a decisive halt at the brink of yet another yawning chasm. Into the abyss, a narrow snow bridge, sunken in the middle like a saddle, led to the other side. The top along its length was a knifelike ridge, an inverted "V" so narrow that the sledge runners would not grip. The sledge would have to be dragged along it, inch by inch.

In a sense, the decision to take this enormous risk was made for them; there was no other option. Lashly went first, with the alpine rope tied about his waist, straddling the bridge's swaybacked spine as he would a horse, and shuffling his way along, not daring to look into the awful void that lay to either side. Under the weight of this one man, the bridge held. The rope was long enough—barely—to give him scope to climb up the snowbank that rose at the opposite end. Gaining its slight summit, he turned toward his companions. Across the gulf, Crean and Lt. Evans could see his face gone white with fear. Now it was their turn. They wasted no time.

They sat face-to-face astride the bridge, with the sledge between them, its runners just resting on the snow on either side. The blue depths of the chasm dropped away beneath their feet. The slightest shift of balance, or the collapse of the bridge with two men and a heavy sledge on it, would doom them all. One slip, one false move, and the sledge and all their hopes with it would go tumbling into the abyss. There was no panic—only a quickly-laid plan, a few well-chosen moves, and the sledge was secured.

They took a moment to look around; there was no way out of the maze. The three men sat wearily on the sledge: they were well and truly done in, and there was not a single ledge wide enough to hold the tent. They had worked all this day without food, saving their last bits until the starkest necessity drove them to eat. Evans went on alone, looking for a way out. How frail and insignificant he looked, and he was their only hope in the immensity of this wilderness.

He returned after an hour, bearing good news. There were some rough patches yet to cross, but they had made it to the bottom of the icefall. Threading along the path he'd found, they emerged that afternoon onto the smooth ice of the glacier. Lashly had been hoarding oddments of food from their regular ration for just such a time, and produced a modest supper. Here they ate the last of their biscuits, and everything else but a little tea and sugar. They were within an easy downhill march of the Middle Glacier Depot. Once there, they camped and had another meal, this time a full one. Replete and relieved, the three men crawled into their reindeer-fur bags and were quickly sound asleep.

Determined to make a better show with the next day's march, they covered twenty miles (32 km) on ski and reached the Lower Glacier Depot at the end of the march a half-day ahead of schedule. The three men had improved on the work allotted to four, and now stood every chance of making it home in good time, perhaps even ahead of schedule.

The Barrier, now so close at hand, had somehow the feel of

home. Three hundred and sixty miles (580 km) still lay between the three men and ultimate safety, but the old familiar Barrier promised a straightforward and level road, and better weather than the stiff plateau wind that must be even now battering away at Scott's Polar Party.

It's your call

(The continuation of the story told in the opening paragraphs of this book.)

They were off the glacier; the hard way now lay behind, and a long straight road before. But their elation would not last long. In camp that night, Lt. Evans complained for the first time of stiffness at the backs of his knees. Any sailor worth his salt knows this is one of the first signs of scurvy. Crean and Lashly had noted their officer's general decline in recent weeks, and now began to secretly examine his gums as he spoke, looking for the telltale swelling and discoloration there. For the time, they kept their concern between themselves.

Looseness of the bowels was beginning to afflict the lieutenant, interrupting the march along the homeward track. He was clearly weakening, complaining daily of stiffness in his legs, and of his skin turning black and blue and other colors as well. The effects of scurvy as it ravages the body include a weakness and lassitude that renders a man helpless, and a swelling in the joints that will cripple before it kills. The skin turns all colors; teeth fall from their sockets.

The two sailors now made clear to Evans what they had long suspected; their words confirmed his own suspicions. This bad news was coupled with a shortage of oil in the tins uncovered at the Mid-Barrier Depot. They could be sure that none of the previous returning parties would have taken more than their share. (It was later determined that the seals on the canisters were damaged by the prolonged cold when buried in the depot.) Taking the barest minimum of oil for their own needs, they left the rest for the returning Polar Party and headed out again.

Evans' condition and the pain it brought grew worse by the day, but he was still able to pull the sledge—barely—in his harness. He suffered his agony in silence, keeping up a cheery front for the benefit of his tent-mates. By now he was passing large amounts of blood daily. Even so, they had been making good mileages—sixteen, fourteen, thirteen, thirteen—but this, too, began to diminish.

On the morning of February 3, still well south of the plenty that lay ahead at One Ton Depot, Evans was barely able to stand without help. Crean and Lashly lifted him and strapped his feet into his skis. The south wind was a help, but even so their daily distances were not enough to assure a safe arrival for all three, with still 180 miles (290 km)—only two more Sundays—to Hut Point.

They made One Ton Depot, the last major port of call before Hut Point, in the late afternoon of February 9. Here they had a last change of diet, a good feed of oatmeal, and at last a surplus of fuel over which to stir their hooshes to a proper boiling. They loaded the sledge with nine days' provisions; no more. Only Crean and Lashly were pulling at all now. Evans was walking slowly alongside the sledge, silent in his pain, alone in his thoughts. He required help to attend to the simplest of matters—even to get into or out of the tent.

As their own pace slowed, the certainty grew in them that the five-man Polar Party, now homeward bound, must be steadily gaining on them. Evans did his best to keep up and vowed to do so until the very end, but all knew he would have to ride on top of the sledge before long. In the long marches they were still pulling in eleven miles (17 km), but it was a struggle for two men. Eleven miles a day might not get them home in time.

On February 12th, the smoking summit of Mount Erebus (the second highest volcano in Antarctica) appeared on the horizon ahead. The image did not last; its encouragement was not enough to keep Evans from fainting more than once, to be revived with difficulty by a drop of brandy. The following day he could not go on. He begged his two companions to save themselves and leave him to his fate. Then as their commanding officer, he *ordered* them to do so.

Had you been Lt. Evans, would you have had the bravery to order your men to save themselves while they could, and leave you to your fate?

It might be mutiny to disobey a direct order, but Crean and Lashly would hear nothing of it: "We shall stand by him to the end, so we are the masters today." After a council of war they concluded to drop by the wayside everything they could possibly get along without, and go on with only the tent, sleeping bags, cooker, and what little food and oil was left. They would carry Lt. Evans on the sledge, and win through all three, or not at all.

Carrying Evans on the sledge this way would slow the party's progress to the point that it might very well leave them stranded without food or oil, to slowly starve out on the Barrier. No one would be coming to rescue them in the short term. If Scott and the Polar Party had successfully reached the South Pole, they would still be too far behind Evans, Crean and Lashly to reach them in time.

This was a brave yet highly risky decision. Lieutenant Evans was likely to die anyway. Knowing that, would you have acted as Crean and Lashly—reducing your own likelihood of surviving to save a dying man?

Do the best you can with what you've got

It added hours to the day's work, to break down the tent around Evans and get him ready to lie on the sledge. Longer hours on the march gave some progress, but at a pitiful rate, even with the help of a sail attached to the top of the sledge and favorable winds. During the heavy drag of February 16, Castle Rock and Observation Hill came occasionally into view. They were close to home, and looking for relief from the dog teams, but there would be no dogs. They would have to make it in under their own steam, even on half-rations.

What a pleasant surprise it was to see the last abandoned,

broken-down motor sledge announcing Corner Camp just ahead. Crean and Lashly uncovered Lt. Evans enough to let him have a look. They picked up some biscuits at the camp, but that was all. With lower temperatures all the time and Evans so weak, they were almost afraid to go to sleep that night for fear he'd freeze.

He hadn't frozen to death when they awoke the next morning, but he was so weak as to be totally helpless, and when Lashly tried to move him he fainted dead away. Crean saw the collapse and thought he had died outright. It was all too much—they'd come so far together, and faced so many hardships, to have it come to this. There were still a few drops of brandy in the medicine chest, just enough to bring him around one last time.

Clearly Evans could not be moved again. They'd come to the end of their food; one more day's oil remained. They'd made the long journey, advanced the Polar Party to within striking distance of the goal, and returned thus far, only to be waylaid by misfortune and stranded hopelessly on this desolate ice plain.

Crean and Lashly stood outside the tent and talked over what to do next. The hut was thirty-five miles (56 km) farther on. Someone might be waiting there, ready with the dog teams to come out to meet the Polar Parties surely close at hand, to help them in. Just as likely, the hut might be empty, and the relief parties still waiting at Cape Evans farther north, assured by recent reports that both Polar Parties were going strong, and able to return home under their own steam.

Although it was risky for anyone to set out alone on this last thirty-five miles, the odds were better than the certain death that would occur for all three by remaining in camp. They had reached the limit of their common endurance. Little food remained for them, and only the merest glimmer of oil for the lamp. Left alone in the tent, Evans would surely, and quickly, die. The other two were almost equal in their waning strength, diminished as it was from the hardy manhood of but a few months past. Together they might have made it in, but neither would agree to leave their lieutenant behind alone to die.

What would you have done?

Crean and Lashly decided that one man must go forward to get what help there may be, or quite literally die trying. For them, it mattered little who drew the short straw, and who the long—who died on the trail, and who in the tent with Lt. Evans. Thirty-five more miles to the hut demanded more strength than either of them could muster. Still, no British seaman would, or could, forget this admonition from the English Admiral Lord Nelson, in the 1700s: "Do the best you can with what you've got." One man would go forward and bring back aid or die in the attempt.

Three biscuits

Crean was the one to go on. He made his farewells—they might well have been his last—to Bill Lashly the stout-hearted stoker, and Lt. Evans, too sick to come to the tent's door to wave goodbye. Two sticks of chocolate and three biscuits in his pocket were all he took. Whether or not it was enough he would find out, but it mattered little. There was not another ounce of food to be taken for the journey. With no tent and no sleeping bag, if Crean stopped for an extended rest along the way, he would likely die in his sleep from exposure and frostbite.

He stopped, as he supposed, near the halfway point. The chocolate in his outer pocket was frozen hard as a brick, and broke up like sand in his parched mouth. He sat down on the snow to rest his legs, but Tom Crean wasn't done yet.

If he weakened and fell short on this final stretch, if he stopped to rest a moment and fell asleep, if a blizzard closed over him and blotted out the light one final fatal time, then so be it. Who was he to challenge God's will? But it was Crean's will now, and it was one foot in front of the other with only another fifteen level miles (24 km) left to go. What were they to the almost fifteen hundred (2,400 km) out-and-back already done?

Five hours of steady going later, he passed Safety Camp. Behind, the weather was beginning to come on thick. No time to slow up now. As he headed toward Cape Armitage, the wind and snow were increasing. He felt, rather than saw, the surface slush he was walking into. Better to try again to scout out a way up and over the gap between Observation Hill and Castle Rock after all, or he'd never get in. He managed—barely—and through rifts in the ragged drift he made out the hut in the distance. There was no sign of life; no sledges or dogs in sight. The place might well be cold and empty, but it lay just ahead. A few more steps and he was at the door.

Edward Atkinson and Dmitri Gerof were warming themselves by the blubber fire inside, listening to the rising wind, and glad they were safe and secure. It looked to be a long hard blow coming on; outside the dogs began their infernal howl. Suddenly Crean appeared at the wooden door and took them by surprise—the supporting party was not unexpected, and anyone on the trail would surely be holed up in his tent for a blow like this. He was covered with new-blown snow, thin and ragged and barely recognizable, "Crean!" They swung the door wide and ushered him in.

Outside the wind kicked up fiercely, battering at the wooden walls of the hut, but sparing the weary traveler home from the trail. No sooner was he safely inside than the storm buried the hut in a whirl of drift. Despite the desperate situation of Evans and Lashly out on the Barrier, there would be no going out to save them until this blizzard subsided. Crean had done all that a man could do.

All day and night until the next morning, the blizzard surged around the hut. The three men drew close to the blubber stove and worried over the fate of the two still out on the Barrier. By afternoon, the storm had abated enough for the doctor and Dmitri to make a start with the dogs, leaving Crean—who wished to go but was ordered to stay behind—alone in the hut.

On the afternoon of February 22, Crean saw the rescue party, their mission accomplished, come round Cape Armitage and clatter up to the hut. Lashly was all right, but Lt. Evans was nearer death than a man had any right to expect a return from. He had suffered greatly bumping over the ice on the road home, but having come this far, amazingly, he would survive. Their terrible ordeal was over, and the success of the great endeavor assured. After a brief reunion and a short rest for the dogs, Crean and Gerof were off for the warmth and plenty at Cape Evans Hut. Lieutenant Evans would need a few more days' lie-in before he could travel again.

Lessons learned

Lieutenant Evans later said that the refusal of Crean and Lashly to leave him to die on the ice was the only time in his military career that anyone had defied a direct order. To have done so would be considered mutiny, yet these two men held their duty to him as their friend higher than their duty to him as commander. Evans dedicated his 1921 book about the expedition, *South with Scott*, to Crean and Lashly.

It is amazing the power that exists within us. Like Crean, we all have hidden reserves of physical strength, bravery and mental willpower, all the more powerful when coupled with a desire to not let one's friends down.

A memorable footnote to this story: when Crean was about halfway through his march he sat down to eat some food. He put one of the three biscuits back in his pocket. Later, when asked why,

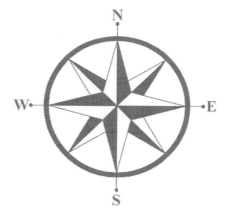

Promises, Promises

How good are you at keeping yours?

he simply replied that he was, *saving it for an emergency.*

A t a young age we learn the importance of promises. As we grow older we discover there are many types of promises: promises to friends or work colleagues; promises to spouses; promises of a financial nature such as a mortgage or loan.

However, in the process of growing up we also learn that it is okay to occasionally break promises. Circumstances change; everyone understands that. With the best intentions, in today's world, we can easily say one thing and mean another, and not feel bad doing so. Politicians do this on a regular basis. On a personal level, how many of us have made a promise to our spouse or partner to come home from work on time, only to break it when an important customer needed attending to?

Rarely do such modern day broken promises so impact another person that they result in their death or suffering. Nowadays, at worst, most broken promises might result in hurt feelings, a damaged relationship, or a financial penalty—but not life or death.

However, life or death is exactly what Shackleton's Ross Sea

Party faced in 1914 and 1915—an impossible task, an unbreakable commitment, and with many lives in the balance, including their own, all depending on the decisions they made.

As described in Chapter 3, after the South Pole was conquered by Amundsen, Shackleton sought a new Antarctic challenge: to be the first to walk *across* continental Antarctica.

His Imperial Trans-Antarctic Expedition plan would require two ships. The *Endurance*, leaving from South Georgia, near South America, would carry Shackleton and his team to the Weddell Sea side of Antarctica. The *Aurora,* leaving from Australia, would take another party, led by Aeneas Mackintosh, to the Ross Sea area on the opposite side. The plan seemed simple enough—Mackintosh and his men would lay depots from the Ross Sea toward the South Pole, so Shackleton and his men, who were going to trek across Antarctica, could pick up food and supplies once they had passed the South Pole and were homeward bound.

In reading the Ross Sea Party's awe-inspiring story, consider what you would have done. Would you have risked everything to keep *your* promise to Shackleton?

A shared understanding

Promises and commitments are the outward signs of mutual trust between parties, a shared understanding, and a bargain to be upheld at each end. This was especially true before the dawn of instantaneous radio communication, when months might elapse between the writing of a letter and its delivery, and between the making of a promise and its fulfilment.

A contract might be drafted to spell out the particulars of an agreement—*who* should have delivered *what* by some specified *date*—but there was more to the commitment than the paper it was written on. There was a sense of honor between the parties that transcended the written contract—that the keeping of one's word after the handshake was, or should be, all that was needed.

Thus, in 1914 it was relatively simple for Shackleton to arrange

—through Aeneas Mackintosh—the purchase of Mawson's wooden ship the *Aurora*. Mawson had just returned from his Australian Antarctic Expedition and at that moment the ship was being refit in Hobart, Tasmania. A proven Antarctic vessel, she would be the ideal ship for use by the Ross Sea section of the Imperial Trans-Antarctic Expedition. Shackleton and Mackintosh were old friends and experienced hands at this exploring business through their shared experiences on Shackleton's 1907-1909 *Nimrod* Expedition.

The plan for the Ross Sea Party of the Imperial Trans-Antarctic Expedition was to land the *Aurora* on Ross Island at the site of the old Discovery Hut built by Scott's 1901-1904 expedition. Using that as a base, Mackintosh and his men, supported by a team of dogs, would then lay a series of supply depots along the trail from the Discovery Hut to the base of the Beardmore Glacier some four hundred miles (640 km) south towards the Pole.

Shackleton and the men who would traverse the continent with him depended for their survival on these supplies being in the designated locations along the Great Ice Barrier. Failure in any part of this plan would doom them to starvation on the ice.

The plan was deceptively simple. Past experience had shown that with proven leadership, a solid team and a bit of luck, a trans-continental journey could be done. All that would be needed for Mackintosh to complete his part would be to obtain the necessary gear and supplies to stock the depots, a number of good men to lay them, and the use of the *Aurora* to get them from Tasmania to Ross Island in the Antarctic and back. It would not be easy, but great plans rely on great expectations.

The two men parted ways in London in September 1914, bound for opposite ends of the Earth, each to the intended completion of his part of the bargain, never to meet again. For his part, Shackleton's *Endurance* was crushed by the shifting ice of the Weddell Sea, as described in Chapter 3: *What Do You Do When Luck Runs Out?* Shackleton failed to land his Trans-Continental Party, but Mackintosh was never to know that. They had no radio or other long-distance communication arranged. The promise had been made, and it was now Mackintosh's job and duty to fulfil it.

Mackintosh arrived in Australia the second week of October 1914 to find that Shackleton had been lax in holding up his own end—promised funds were sadly lacking, and the ship was in a poor state of repair. The scientists who were to have rounded out the *Aurora*'s staff were actually aboard the *Endurance* that was bound for the Weddell Sea with Shackleton; some of the seamen whose names were on the *Aurora* roster were nowhere to be found. Shackleton's agents in London were uncooperative and unwilling to release funds (which were in fact not available.)

But Mackintosh had given his word. There was no question of yielding to this inadequate support. So began a long cascade of decisions playing out over many months and thousands of miles, all of them aimed toward one overarching goal—making the Ross Sea side of the expedition successful. Regardless of the untenable situation facing Mackintosh in Tasmania, Shackleton's Trans-Antarctic overland party would be looking for their depots, possibly as early as the coming Antarctic autumn. Mackintosh immediately began networking and fundraising, and in the end cobbled together enough of everything needed to set sail on December 23, 1914. A few weeks late, but still in time—barely—to get at least a few of the depots laid out upon the South Polar Trail.

A question of authority

Mackintosh had an invaluable ally to help wring success out of the confusion reigning in Tasmania. Ernest Joyce was the one true Antarctic veteran on hand. He had first been south with Scott's *Discovery* Expedition, and then again with Shackleton's *Nimrod* Expedition. He was a well-established handler for the eighteen dogs that would accompany Mackintosh to the Ross Sea. Joyce was also familiar with the specialized stores and equipment of a polar expedition. Unlike Mackintosh, who was a seasoned ship's captain and chosen leader of the Ross Sea Party, Joyce for all his braggadocio and his sea and sledging experience, had no instinctive capacity for leadership. The two men found themselves in a sometimes uneasy partnership, directing the work of the unlikely team brought together in the port of Hobart, Tasmania.

Their work was hindered from the beginning by the lack of funds, insufficient supplies, and the late start. These were factors whose ultimate consequences had yet to be fully realized. The primary, unavoidable decision was this: they would keep their promise and on no account would Shackleton's overland party be abandoned to their fate.

Upon landing at Ross Island

Some, but not all of the necessary stores were landed at Discovery Hut, and the Ross Sea Party managed to place them in depots as far south as the waning season would allow, seventy miles (112 km) to the distinctive headland known as Minna Bluff. These preliminary advance depots were intended to support the real work of the expedition to be undertaken in the following spring—the laying of well-stocked depots all the way to the Beardmore Glacier.

Given the late departure from Hobart, there was simply not enough time to do more for Shackleton's overland party. It was believed—and fervently hoped—that Shackleton would have been similarly delayed on his own start, and not be coming over this same autumn.

Despite the occasional clash of their towering egos, Mackintosh and Joyce were in general agreement as to the details being worked out as the expedition progressed. When they were not, Mackintosh's will, and his official and natural position as leader of the party, held sway. In the first depot-laying foray, the captain was anxious to lay in as much as he could, as quickly and as far south as possible in case Shackleton had made an early start and was already on his way.

Mackintosh wanted to take all the dogs right away, hauling overloaded sledges. Joyce wanted to take only the fittest dogs and use lightly loaded sledges to get the dogs acclimated to hard work after their long sea voyage. He feared the loss of the dogs if they were not correctly handled at this critical time.

The aftermath of this journey proved Joyce right. Mackintosh, being the nominal leader, had his way, but he was proving ever more ineffectual as the leader of the party. Only four dogs survived to aid in the next season's depot work.

Unavoidable circumstances

Some decisions must be made in the face of unavoidable circumstances. The first big obligation so blithely taken back in London could not be kept exactly as committed. The time had run out before the furthest depots could be placed, and the money had run out too. The decision had long ago been made to winter the ship in the Antarctic, and there were simply no funds to support a return to the warmer climate of Tasmania until the following spring.

No one thought this was a good idea; the ship might easily become trapped, possibly crushed, or just as likely carried away by the pace of the drifting ice. But the die had been cast. As far as they knew, Shackleton and his men were on their way from the Weddell Sea and starting their walk across the continent. There would be no turning back for Shackleton, as there was no way Mackintosh could warn Shackleton or his team if the Ross Sea Party depots were not laid. It was risky to keep the *Aurora* in the ice off Cape Evans, tethered to the shore by a web of steel cables, but in the face of all other sacrifices it seemed there was no other option.

Although it might have been gambling with the fate of the ship and every man in the Ross Sea Party, Mackintosh and the *Aurora*'s master, J. R. Stenhouse, agreed that it must be done. Previous experience, limited though it was, indicated that the winter ice off Cape Evans could be expected to remain fast until spring. Lying quietly just offshore, the ship would serve as a warehouse for the supplies yet to be landed. With enough steel cables to anchors deep-set in the gravel shore the ship ought to be safe, so most of the necessary gear and supplies were left on board.

But she was not, although everything had seemed safe and secure, and going according to plan. When the first depot-laying parties set off for the south on January 25, 1915, the *Aurora* was anchored in open water just offshore. During their absence, the ice froze solid around her.

Changing plans

Until, that is, the morning of May 7, 1915 after a severe blizzard, when R.W. Richards stepped outside the hut and looked up to see that the ship was gone. Open water lapped at the previously iced-in beach. The ice had gone out in one vast, solid sheet overnight, taking the *Aurora* and most of the shore party's provisions with it.

The men on shore were marooned for at least a season and possibly more. The tents, the bulk of their provisions, the Primus stoves, the sleeping bags, and everything absolutely necessary to spend months in the field laying more depots had gone with the ship. For all they knew, the ship could have been crushed by the ice and sunk. The hope of rescue was slim; word of their fate might be years getting out.

They had no way of knowing that the *Aurora* was still afloat and would remain stuck in the ice for another nine months; she moved slowly northwest with the drifting ice, powerless to escape, with tons of now useless sledging gear and rations neatly stowed in her hold. She, at least, was relatively safe.

There were ten men stuck on shore now; six of whom were still on their depot journey. They had enough on hand to get by, themselves. But there was nowhere near enough to support the overland journeys required in the spring, to create and stock the depots for Shackleton. Yet a promise had been made. Regardless of circumstances, Mackintosh and his men agreed it must be kept.

Reunited again in the hut at Cape Evans, they had the winter to figure out a way to keep that promise. First came the inventory. As previously noted, every sailor among them knew well the Admiral Lord Nelson's admonition, "Do the best you can with what you've got." What *did* they have? They raided the nearby huts—

Shackleton's 1907 hut at Cape Royds and Scott's 1901 one at Hut Point—and gathered every item of any value. This included bolts of canvas, balding sleeping bags, battered Primus stoves, worn-out sledges, decade-old biscuits and dried preserved sledging food— everything that could be restored for use in the big push in the spring. Through their ingenuity and perseverance, they were able to develop enough food and supplies to stock a series of depots all the way to the Beardmore Glacier. Amazingly, all was going according to the plans originally made by Shackleton back in England.

Meeting the promise would still be a massive challenge. It would take a great deal of effort for ten men to take on the work of *twice* their number, with four dogs standing in for the original nine that survived the voyage down, and with salvaged, damaged and worn equipment scavenged from three previous expeditions.

More was about to be demanded of them than anyone had anticipated. All the men ashore had joined the expedition with a good idea of what would be expected, and had accepted their positions and hazardous duty pay based on that understanding. Now they needed to do so much more work, at a greater personal risk. Looking at this from a cost-benefit ratio perspective, that ratio must now be recast in a different light. A sense of ultimate adventure and the reward of being part of a noble and heroic undertaking had now become overshadowed by the formidable task of moving tons of supplies hundreds of miles with far too few resources to sustain the effort.

At what point would lesser men have thrown in the towel, and accepted that they could not fulfil their promise? No one in the hut that winter fully appreciated the sacrifices that would have to be made to keep their promise, but surely they must have had an inkling of the difficulty.

A promise made is a promise kept

The fulfilment of their promise was the result of a series of conscious decisions made on the spot: what must be done, how can it be done with the resources at hand, who will be the ones to go out onto the trail, and when will they begin? Such decisions are identical to those that are made countless times, in the everyday lives of countless people and in ongoing business decisions that in the end result in profit or loss, success or failure. We have an idea of what we must do, and an inventory of what is at hand to do it.

There was never a discussion of facing up to the reality of the situation, and reneging on their promise. The commitment to others was too great to ignore, but there were additional forces at work. They must work together to do their level best to get the job done, or bear the weight of guilt for not having tried hard enough. There were also obligations to the expedition and to the sacrifices great and small of every man involved, as well as to the higher purpose of exploration and discovery. Each man looked deep into his own heart and found his own answers. They were remarkably united in purpose.

After careful consideration over the course of that first winter, it became clear that everyone must pull his own weight equally to get the job done. The stores must be advanced in successive relays, by three-man teams. The distances were such that no single team could take a load for the whole distance; no fewer than three teams would be needed. Nine out of the ten men must be away in the field; the last must be content to wait behind, alone for upwards of four months, while the others completed the work. The sheer bravery of what they planned is still admired, more than a hundred years after the event.

Anything less than total unity of purpose would have doomed this plan, its participants, and the lives of those coming overland relying on its completion. The psychological factor of apparently unanimous and unconditional support cannot be underestimated. More than a matter of mere group-think, it can play a defining role in group decision making no matter what the era or import of the decision. Not one of these ten men would want to be forever known as the shirker who declined to take on his equal share of the effort and the risk to fulfil the promise.

In an interesting contrast, one might ask how a *modern* team would have coped. Would contemporary values of diversity of thought have led to insurmountable conflicts, and in the end, a failure to carry out the mission's vital goal?

Best balance of skills

Their plan was that the nine fittest men would take on the sledging job, leaving Alexander Stevens alone in the hut to keep the meteorological records at Cape Evans. Three teams of three men each would take to the field as early as possible to sledge the depot supplies overland four hundred miles (644 km) to the mouth of the Beardmore Glacier. With so few men, and the bare minimum of sledging equipment and supplies for themselves, the plan would be extremely dangerous. The breakdown of any one of the three Primus stoves would doom the men in that tent to a cold death on the Barrier. If one man succumbed to frostbite or scurvy, the others in his team would have to decide whether to carry on, or retreat to save their own lives at the expense of Shackleton and his team, who would search in vain for depots that were never laid.

By the time spring arrived, each was ready to risk all to do his part. Whatever reservations any one of them had felt about the upcoming campaign were now submerged beneath the group decision to do their utmost to lay the depots. In early spring—too early, in the bitterly cold September of 1915—all the available resources were gathered at Hut Point, and the long process of conveying two thousand pounds of food and fuel over the Barrier began. Each three-man team would drag a heavy load forward over the Barrier, then go back for another. The three teams leapfrogged each other in parallel routes, sometimes in company, but more often isolated and on their own.

The three teams were chosen as far as practicable to have the best balance of skills—polar experience, physical durability, and leadership capacity—but there was not much to choose from. Ninety percent of the staff on hand must be pressed into duty regardless of their skills. Each team's tasks within the overall regime of the depot-laying was much the same: follow the schedule as best you can, do the work assigned to you, and get back safely at the end of it.

Once departed from the hut, each team was entirely on their own. The decisions once made collectively by a group of ten must now be made separately by the men in the three isolated tents. There was an unwavering commitment to the overall task—to lay the depots where they were expected to be found.

To those doing it, the work seemed endless; day after day of slow walking in harness, hauling along a heavily-weighted sledge through a dismal and often obscured landscape of ice. The four dogs remaining were of little real help. Frostbite and snow blindness were a constant risk and caused unending misery. Under duress, the unity was collapsing; disharmony split the parties. Mackintosh forged ahead, leaving Joyce in charge of five other men hauling a staggering load amounting to 232 pounds each.

When their Primus stove broke down, one of the three-man parties was sent back to their base, leaving the other six men to fulfil the promise. Farther out on the Barrier, one of those men, stricken by scurvy, gave out a hundred miles (160 km) short of the Beardmore Glacier. This sick man, Padre Arnold Spencer-Smith, suggested to the others that they ought to leave him behind and continue on to the Beardmore without him. He could stay in one of the two tents, and the other five men would have to crowd into a tent designed for three. It was an awkward plan, but they all agreed to it. Here again was proof that these men considered that a promise made would be a promise kept, regardless of the personal sacrifice. This commitment had become much more than the fulfilment of a contract. It was a matter of honor.

A question of leadership

Another formidable strain on the decision process arose on the Barrier hundreds of miles from home, when the nominal leader of the combined parties, Aeneas Mackintosh, weakened by scurvy, informally handed over the leadership role to Ernest Joyce. For all his experience as a veteran of the Antarctic, Joyce had no inherent capacity for leadership. He was, as he had always been, one of the men and not an officer. He was a sailor who was used to receiving and following orders, not giving them.

Now the others were looking to him for leadership, for a natural capacity to judge not only the nature of the weather and sledging equipment, but also that of the men he was now expected to lead. He was sadly lacking. Still, a void must be filled, and Joyce, with Richards' support and the compliance of Mackintosh and the other two, was the man to fill it.

Thankfully, raw experience in the field would be enough to see all the men back to the hut. All but the Padre who waited for them, alone on the ice, ten thousand miles (16,000 km) from home. Too weakened by scurvy by the time they picked him up on the way back, he died long before they reached home. Months in the field without fresh food will do that to a body. On the journey back, both Mackintosh and Victor Hayward also became too weak to walk. The other three men willingly dragged their near-lifeless bodies on the sledges the last miles to Hut Point.

It was late in the Antarctic autumn, but the sea surface between the Discovery Hut and Cape Evans had not yet frozen. The survivors would have to lay up, surviving on cached frozen seal meat until the sea froze and they could walk across to the much better supplied hut at Cape Evans. Thin weak ice would appear, only to drift away again before it became firm enough to support the weight of a man. The weakened men recovered from the scurvy on their diet of relatively fresh food, and were soon fit enough to consider walking over to Cape Evans as soon as the ice would allow.

Mackintosh, ever headstrong, was anxious to be off. As the officially designated leader, there was no one who could overrule his decisions. He convinced Hayward to join him in the last leg of the depot journey, home to Cape Evans. Joyce, Richards, and Ernest Wild stayed on at the hut, heeding the wisdom of Joyce to wait until the ice was stronger before starting out. The next day Joyce,

Richards and Wild followed the footsteps of their companions out to where they abruptly ended at the edge of the fast ice.

In this sad footnote to the heroic commitment of the Ross Sea Party, two more men were dead, this time due to the ill-considered advice of a man accustomed to the role of leadership but not always able to make the best decisions. There are lessons to be taken here. Ironically *these* were the two men who had been most stricken by scurvy, but were dragged back to safety by Joyce, Richards and Wild, and could have lived to proudly tell the tale of how they had kept their promise to Shackleton.

Keeping the faith

As noted earlier, the *Aurora* did not sink. Encased in ice, she drifted for nine months until that ice broke up and freed her. Damaged from exposure, she eventually made it to New Zealand. The fates of the ten men left marooned at Cape Evans, and of Shackleton, remained for a time unknown to the outside world.

The *Endurance* had been crushed in the ice of the Weddell Sea, but in the end all twenty-eight of her men survived. Their stories can be found in Chapters 3, 5 and 11. After the rescue of his men on Elephant Island, Shackleton found himself unceremoniously relieved of the command of the Ross Sea Party of the expedition. Even so he made it to New Zealand in time to board the *Aurora*, which had safely landed and was now refitted for the relief journey south. She sailed on December 20, 1916. Seven of the ten men of the Ross Sea Party were picked up and lived to come home and tell the tale. The depots that they laid with such great commitment and at such tremendous personal sacrifice remained covered with snow. They had kept their promise to Shackleton.

In looking back at what the Ross Sea Party achieved, it is all the more remarkable to note that when Mackintosh and his men were assembling the provisions and laying the depots for Shackleton's team, despite their own highly limited rations, Mackintosh and his men had at no time dipped into the rations and supplies reserved for Shackleton.

Were their efforts wasted? Those depots, the end result of decisions made to honor a commitment, are an illumination of a higher purpose—that when we have made a promise, we *can* do everything within our power to keep it. The depots remain to this day—unused on the Ross Ice Shelf in Antarctica—a testament to this principle.

By comparison, many of the promises made in our modern lives seem so easy. Would *you* make the sacrifices to fulfil a promise, the way Mackintosh and his men did? Even if you did, how would you feel upon learning that the depots were laid completely in vain, as Shackleton and his men *never* even started their march across Antarctica?

In the next chapter, called, *Do You Agree All Is Fair In Love, War And Polar Exploration?* we'll explore other types of decisions and promises, especially those made between the expedition leaders themselves. As for how Mackintosh's men felt about their great effort in laying the depots that were never to be used, we'll let them

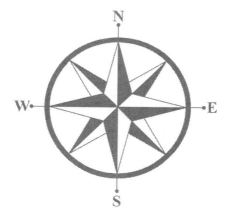

Do You Agree All Is Fair In Love, War And Polar Exploration?

Discovery or victory: the double face of polar exploration.

answer that in Chapter 12, *What Is Your Greater Purpose?*

The grand goals set forth for any expedition are not for the weak of constitution or the faint of heart. The successful leaders of the heroic age had more than just youth, health and a clear goal in mind. They all had ambition, coupled with a very strong sense of personal destiny. Each of them felt that it was his obligation to find his rightful place in history by bringing his discoveries home to a grateful nation.

Such ambition is not to be taken lightly, so it comes as no surprise that when two or more are fighting for the same elusive goal, unseemly competition may dim the lustre of the prize. The outward veneer of gentlemanly disagreement falls by the wayside, and deeper conflicts may come to light.

We are familiar with the expression *all is fair in love and war*. It is easy to understand its sentiment—that in certain circumstances, the rule book can be thrown out. The prize, whether it is a new lover or a military victory, is more important than the rules.

What makes the question, *what is fair?* so interesting is that societal rules (i.e., the "rule book") change over time. Even within the same era, societal mores vary from country to country, and from culture to culture. Context can also change as events unfold—what's acceptable at one point, might not be acceptable "down the road," whether that's measured in distance or time.

Society is based on a set of rules and ethics prescribing acceptable and unacceptable behavior. Courts of law and written constitutions help to spell out what is right and wrong in most situations, but they cannot cover every eventuality. Ultimately it comes down to an unspoken yet common understanding of what is acceptable. What one person might deem as *fair* is open to interpretation by all who view it—those whom it directly affects, those whom it peripherally affects, and those looking at it a hundred years later. Some might claim that the bigger the prize, the more the rule book can be ignored. Others would argue the exact opposite.

In this chapter we lay out four true situations where the explorers of the heroic age may have touched, or gone over, that fine line. What makes these situations stand out is that the men involved in the expeditions seem to have behaved with such remarkable honor and fairness to each other. While the leaders were occasionally rivals, they shared knowledge, and at times even equipment and ships. The *Aurora* was used by both Mawson and later by Shackleton for the Ross Sea Party. The huts left by Scott and Shackleton, and some of the supplies left ashore by them, were put to good use by later expeditions. Amundsen invited the men of Scott's Eastern Party to make their shore station in the area of the Bay of Whales. (They graciously declined and moved northward to become the ill-fated Northern Party described in Chapter 11.)

Experienced leaders gave credit to junior expedition members, senior scientists taught more junior scientists, and people were exceptionally civil to one another despite incredibly trying circumstances. Amazingly, given the duration and challenges of these expeditions, there is surprisingly little history of serious tension among the men. In contrast to other eras of exploration (for example to the Arctic) there were no fistfights, no deliberate sabotage and no attempted murder. Great examples of fairness

Do You Agree All Is Fair In Love, War And Polar Exploration?

117

and generosity, in large measure and in small, were displayed throughout. Among all the men, in all their travails, the reigning spirit was "share and share alike." Scott's and Shackleton's support teams took only their fair share of depot supplies and food, even when they were suffering badly due to starvation, exposure and frostbite.

In deciding where that "fairness" line is and what you might have done in each of these situations, keep in mind the size of the prize: in the early 1900s much of the world had been discovered, and only a few spectacular goals remained to capture the popular imagination. Their attainment would place one's name in the history books *forever*; first to the top of Mount Everest; first to the North Pole; first to the South Pole.

1902-1903: In sickness and in health

On Scott's *Discovery* Expedition, the first of the heroic age, one of the goals was a push south towards the Pole. Scott knew he did not have the resources or experience to actually reach it and get back alive, but with a small team he could achieve a furthest southern point, possibly as far as 85° S, about 350 miles (560 km) from the South Pole. The three-man team—Scott, Dr. Edward Wilson, and Ernest Shackleton—set off in November 1902. Shackleton was the junior member of the team. Prior to departure, signs of his possible ill health—shortness of breath and coughing—had caught the attention of Wilson, but neither he nor Shackleton flagged this weakness to their leader Scott.

Their journey south was challenging. They were encumbered by the heavy load on their sledge, limited rations, and their collective inexperience in controlling unruly dogs. By the time they reached their furthest southern point on December 31, 1902, at 82°17' S (about 530 miles or 850 km from the South Pole), Shackleton's health had deteriorated due to scurvy. On the journey back, he grew weaker and weaker. Wilson thought he might die, but Shackleton's resilient spirit pulled him through. However, at various points on the return journey, Shackleton had to leave the man-hauling of the heavily-laden sledge—challenging enough for a three-man team—to just Scott and Wilson. At times he was so weak and near death, he had to be placed on top of the sledge, adding his own weight to it while the other two pulled it forward. (This situation has shocking similarities to the Crean, Evans and Lashly survival story told in Chapter 7.)

Through perseverance and sheer grit, they all made it back safely to the Discovery Hut after ninety-three days of hazardous travel. Shackleton eventually recovered from scurvy, though he still suffered from shortness of breath. Wilson's health, too, suffered for about a month from the effects of that journey. When Scott was deciding who should go back on the *Morning* (the *Discovery* Expedition relief ship) and who should stay in Antarctica for another season, he insisted that Shackleton should be invalided home, despite the man's keen desire to stay.

Had *you* been Shackleton, with such a desperate desire to go south with Scott and Wilson, would you have hidden your symptoms for as long as possible before the southern journey started?

1907-1908: Is it fair to hold onto a sector of a vast continent?

Shackleton made the most of his early return to Britain. His lectures about the *Discovery* Expedition enthused the public. He was already planning an expedition of his own, soon to be named the British Antarctic Expedition, using the Scottish whaler *Nimrod* with a goal of reaching the South Pole first.

On his own return to Britain, at the end of the *Discovery* Expedition, Scott also began working on plans for another expedition also with the goal of being first to the Pole. Scott also planned to conduct further scientific investigation. Always looking forward, he started working with Reginald Skelton (chief engineer on the *Discovery* Expedition) and others to develop motorized vehicles for travel in the region.

Scott first learned of Shackleton's plan to establish his expedition base at McMurdo Sound, and to re-use Scott's Discovery Hut on Ross Island, in a newspaper report. Shackleton hadn't asked Scott for permission to do so, nor had he sought the approval of the Royal Geographical Society. In response, Scott decided to impose a restriction on where Shackleton could land the *Nimrod*. By laying claim to the Ross Sea/McMurdo Sound sector as his own, he sought to limit Shackleton's choices for an expedition base. Edward Wilson—who knew both men well from their perilous ninety-three-day journey during Scott's *Discovery* Expedition only a few years before—tried to act as an intermediary.

Could Scott really claim to own the rights to McMurdo Sound simply because his *Discovery* Expedition had landed there and built a hut? Could he really prevent Shackleton from using the spot as a base when his own second expedition had yet to be fully funded? If you were Wilson, how would you have brokered a peace between the two explorers?

An exchange of correspondence between Scott, Wilson and Shackleton, helped convince Shackleton that if he did land at McMurdo Sound and make his base there, and his conquest of the Pole was successful, his victory would be tainted because Scott had laid the groundwork.

Shackleton reluctantly agreed. He decided to take the *Nimrod* to King Edward VII Land at the far eastern end of the Great Ice Barrier, even though part of the appeal to his financial backers was that he would start from a known location at Hut Point on Ross Island. The route south from there had already been pioneered, revealing a likely path right to the Pole. Once Shackleton acquiesced to Scott's request, he had to carefully break this news to his current and potential backers.

Upon arriving in the Antarctic region, Shackleton and his *Nimrod* headed for King Edward VII Land. Despite their best efforts, they were unsuccessful in getting the *Nimrod* to penetrate the sea ice there. The inlet in the ice visited by the *Discovery* in 1902 had broken away; it was clearly no safe place to winter over. In the end they felt their *only* choice was to head back to McMurdo Sound and Ross Island. They landed and successfully set up a base at Cape Royds, about eleven miles north (17 km) of Scott's original base.

In fairness to Shackleton, his correspondence to his wife during this time reveals how difficult this decision was for him. He had left Tasmania fully intending to honor his agreement to Scott to avoid McMurdo Sound. It might be considered ironic when one considers that Shackleton was a key member of Scott's original *Discovery* Expedition that established a base there in the first place. However, at the time claims to territory by explorers was considered fair-play. (A good example was Robert Peary's claim to the route he was pioneering to the North Pole.)

In the *all is fair in love and war* world, Scott seemed entitled to make his claim, and clearly Shackleton understood that. In a gentleman's game of exploration, however, he could not make that claim indefinitely. They finally agreed to a three-year window of ownership. The debate continues even a hundred years later. Whose side would you have been on?

There were, however, even greater rivalries emerging in Antarctica ...

1910-1912: Street-fighting lessons in polar exploration

One of the first lessons street fighters learn is that there are no rules. If one waits in a gentlemanly manner for a bell to sound, the other fighter will have already thrown the first punch. A successful street fighter ignores all rules, believing instead that "all is fair in love, war and street fighting" and, without announcement, floors his opponent before the fight has begun.

Roald Amundsen was a polar explorer who approached expeditions with the mind-set of a street fighter. He looked for every angle to get an advantage. That might mean living and dressing like the Canadian Netsilik Inuit people, right down to the fur underwear. Or it might mean learning the best skills from the most experienced people he could find, like the famed Norwegian explorer Fridtjof

Nansen, and Olav Bjaaland, one of Norway's best skiers. Prior to his assault on the South Pole, Amundsen had already achieved fame for leading the first successful navigation of the Northwest Passage in 1903 on board the *Gjøa*.

Amundsen was obsessive about finding the best of everything he required for his expeditions: the right mixture of pemmican to aid digestion, the best skis, boots and bindings, and the best wood for crates to be used on the sledges. When existing equipment, such as snow goggles, failed to meet his exacting standards, he designed new versions himself. Most importantly, he took the time to learn the intricacies of dog sledging. He knew from bitter experience that man-hauling was a highly debilitating means of transport. Dog sledging was a far superior way to travel on snow and ice for long distances. His reputation and experience earned Nansen's respect, and gained him the right to use Nansen's famous ship, the *Fram*.

In early 1909, the North Pole had yet to be discovered. Amundsen was planning another Arctic voyage with the aim of claiming that discovery for himself. His plans were usurped later that year when Peary and Cook both announced their competing claims to having reached the North Pole. Amundsen knew that Scott was planning another attempt on the South Pole, after Shackleton's 1907 *Nimrod* Expedition had tried, and failed, to reach it. (Chapter 10, *Will The Results Be Worth The Effort?* tells the saga of that attempt.)

Keeping his plans secret from his own crew and even from Nansen, Amundsen diverted his ship and its provisions from the Arctic to Antarctica and "challenged" Scott to a race to the South Pole. Scott had no plans for a race. He was on a methodical course of scientific discovery—attempting to reach the South Pole was just one element of his multi-year expedition. With no apparent rivals, he had no reason to pre-empt valuable scientific work to get a head start on the Pole.

Amundsen informed Scott of his intentions through a rather cryptic telegram sent from Madeira that he knew Scott would not receive until arriving in Melbourne, just prior to sailing to Antarctica. It simply said, "Beg leave to inform you *Fram* proceeding

Antarctic.—Amundsen."

There are fascinating comparisons to be made between the leadership styles of Amundsen and Scott, as well as contrasts between preferred modes of transport on the snow and ice. Amundsen believed dogs would be superior to Scott's untried and potentially unreliable motor transports, and his Siberian ponies. The animals required large amounts of fodder to be carried on the sledges, and on particularly cold and windy evenings after a hard day of sledging, the men had to expend valuable additional energy building snow walls to shelter them. (The ponies had the unfortunate habit of sometimes kicking the walls over in the middle of the night, forcing the men to get up to rebuild them.) In contrast, Amundsen's dogs all had thick fur coats and were comfortable sleeping directly on the snow. Being carnivores, they could be fed from the dead carcasses of the other dogs, as some dogs weakened and died.

Despite Amundsen's telegram, Scott stuck to his timetable and maintained his scientific exploration. He allowed three of his more important men, Wilson, Bowers and Cherry-Garrard, to go on a perilous winter journey to retrieve emperor penguin eggs, with the goal of verifying an important scientific theory that the embryos would reveal the missing link between reptilian dinosaurs and birds. Their story is told in Chapter 12, *What Is Your Higher Purpose?* The great danger, risks and hardships of a mid-winter excursion meant that these three men would have only three months to recover from this "worst journey in the world" before setting out with Scott on the final assault on the Pole. Surely, had Scott really been in a race, he would have made sure that his best men were fully rested through the exceptionally cold and dark winter months for a strong start on the Pole as soon as spring came. Isn't that what you would have done?

Was Amundsen being *fair* to Scott to pre-announce his intention to also head to Antarctica, or was he goading Scott into a race that Scott was unprepared for? Do you think he was playing games with Scott by sending him that cryptic telegram—which didn't exactly state his real intention of getting to the Pole first—or would it have been better not to tell Scott at all?

At least Amundsen hadn't attempted to land in McMurdo Sound and challenge Scott's claim to that location. The two expeditions could work independently of each other, each focused on its own goals—Amundsen to reach the Pole first, Scott to reach the Pole first and do the finest scientific work. The outcome is one of the most famous and ironic stories in the history of exploration.

If you were Amundsen would you have pre-announced your intentions? If you were Scott, and had received Amundsen's telegram, would you have changed your plans and raced to the Pole?

1911: A simple message to be returned

Amundsen and his team arrived at the South Pole on December 14, 1911, more than a month ahead of Scott and his team. Amundsen spent several days marking out the Pole as far as ten miles (16 km) in all directions. Recognizing the controversy surrounding Cook's and Peary's disputed claims to the North Pole, Amundsen wanted to be as precise and clear as possible that he had indeed found the exact, most southern spot on the planet, given the potential inaccuracies in their measuring equipment. Upon leaving the South Pole, Amundsen left a tent, a Norwegian flag, some discarded equipment, and one letter for Scott, and another for the King of Norway to be delivered by Scott.

It was reasonable for Amundsen to go to great lengths to prove that he was first and he had accurately located it. One can assume that Scott would have done the same had he arrived first, as the pinpoint spot of the South Pole was elusive given the navigational equipment of the era. It is also fully understandable why Amundsen would leave a Norwegian flag. Scott was carrying a British flag for the same purpose, to be left flying at the South Pole, proof that he had reached it first.

However, when the return journey requires many hundreds of miles of sledging across rough terrain, one might think that the letter to the King of Norway that was left for Scott was a way of Amundsen rubbing his victory in Scott's face. What was fair in those circumstances?

Was that letter for the King of Norway a psychological game that Amundsen was playing with Scott, in the same way Amundsen's cryptic telegram announcing his decision to go south was? Or was the letter just recognition that after the dispute over the North Pole, there had to be some secondary proof of goal attainment, and what better way than from the only other human beings who had ever ventured this far in this hostile terrain? Perhaps this was Amundsen's way of saying that if he and his men did not make it back, (if they fell victim to blizzards, crevasses, scurvy, or any of a myriad of dangers they all faced), that this letter would be indisputable proof that he had achieved his goal and conquered the South Pole in the name of Norway.

Amundsen's actions may have been "victory insurance" or a subtle means of damaging the morale of his rival, or both. After all, some people might believe that in an "all is fair in love and war" scenario, it's not sufficient to win, unless you crush your opponent in the process. What would you have done if you were Amundsen? If you were Scott, would you have kept Amundsen's letter and delivered it as requested, or would you have been angered by Amundsen's use of you as a courier from the most desolate place on Earth? Would you have ripped it to pieces and scattered it to the south polar winds? In the end Scott, chose the honorable act—he kept Amundsen's letter with the intention of delivering it, had he survived.

There is an interesting and touching footnote to the story of this letter. It was found among Scott's possessions when the tent containing the remains of Scott, Bowers and Wilson was discovered the following spring. The letter was finally delivered by Lt. Evans, the officer who was saved by Tom Crean's courageous thirty-five mile "do or die trying" march (described in Chapter 7). Evans brought the letter to the King of Norway in person. On that trip, Lt. Evans met a Norwegian woman, fell in love, and married her.

They would not have met had Scott discarded Amundsen's letter.

Rivalries all involved Scott

One of the common denominators of all four "all's fair in love and war" situations is that they all involved Scott. Was this because of Scott's personality, or the fact that he led the first heroic age expedition and became the man to beat? His 1901-1904 *Discovery* Expedition set the framework of how an expedition could combine geological, meteorological, oceanographic, and other scientific pursuits with the adventure and excitement of geographical discovery.

Did the expedition leaders get too close to that unique point where "all is fair in love and war?" Would you have done any differently? In your own personal and business life, have you gotten too close to the line sometimes?

* * *

The next chapter describes one of the most intriguing life and death decisions ever made on a heroic age expedition. Would you make the decision to achieve your goal, knowing full well that once you reached it, you were certain to die before getting back to

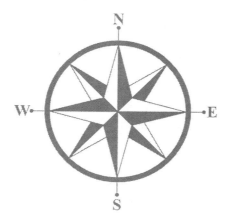

Will The Results Be Worth The Effort?

Going the distance to find out.

civilization?

Setting the goal.

Humans possess an awareness of the future and it is this awareness that enables us to plan. We are goal-driven, social animals, and we can individually and collectively plan today what we desire our future to be.

All of us have something in our lives that remains undone, something that we see for our own futures, to which we aspire, and to which we assign some part of each day's endeavor. The goal might be lofty or it might be mundane, but it lies before us, yet to be accomplished. Perhaps it is at the limit of our ability, just out of reach.

Having set that goal, the next task is to go for it—set out on the path we believe will take us there—and go the distance.

Shackleton's plans

Let us go back in time, to journey with Ernest Shackleton towards the South Pole in 1908. Over a hundred years ago, he knew that the South Pole of the Earth had yet to be discovered—that is, visited in the flesh—and that *he* would be the one to do it. That goal became his life's aim, to which he then directed all of his energies.

Now, this is a grand goal, one that takes a great deal of ambition to conceive, and a great deal of personal and collective effort to accomplish. After all the planning and preparation, the ocean voyages, and landing on the icebound shores of Antarctica, only then—or so it may seem—did the real work of discovery begin. Still ahead lay the months of trudging many hundreds of miles over vast tracts of ice and snow, all to plant the nation's flag on a featureless plain on a point identified only by navigational coordinates.

It was a patriotic goal of considerable importance, one that would greatly enhance national pride, while also achieving scientific results and the geographic discovery of this last unknown place, and what was to be found there. But more importantly, for Shackleton it was a personal goal. It was what induced him to risk his fortune, his reputation, and his life, in what he envisioned as a shared victory.

But the most powerful force driving his efforts to take the Pole with his *Nimrod* Expedition was an unyielding personal ambition. The sting of having been invalided home (described in Chapter 9), after his breakdown during the southern advance of Scott's *Discovery* Expedition, was almost more than he could bear. Following his quick recovery from the ravages of exposure and scurvy, he immediately set about planning and bringing together his own Antarctic expedition, subject to no one's control but his own.

This time, come what may, he was bound to take the South Pole at last, as much for himself and his wounded pride as for the British flag under which his expedition sailed.

The Nimrod Expedition: 1907-1909

Shackleton's years of planning finally took shape in the form of his ship the *Nimrod* and her long voyage from England to Antarctica. After a fruitless search for a landing place near King Edward VII Land, he and his men landed their stores and set up camp on Ross

Island at a rocky point of land named Cape Royds. The landing place was not ideal for the task at hand. The thirty miles (48 km) of sea ice blocking the ship's path to Hut Point—another thirty miles farther south—would have to remain in place until the following spring. Without this transitory ice highway, the ponies, and the expedition, would remain stuck at Cape Royds, unable to move. As the *Discovery* had found, the fickle ways of the sea ice could neither be predicted, nor overcome by force or wishful thinking.

On October 29, 1908, Shackleton was poised for a start. He set off with three additional men (Jameson Adams, Eric Marshall, and Frank Wild) on what he knew would be a historic journey. They carried with them 784 pounds of provisions, drawn by the four remaining ponies on four eleven-foot sledges, enough for ninety-one days of hard traveling to get them to the South Pole and back. If they could maintain an average speed of nineteen miles (30 km) per day—over the known level of the Barrier and the unknown beyond—they would reach the mythical spot itself. A separate party including Douglas Mawson, Edgeworth David and Alistair Mackay, would head west to discover the South Magnetic Pole. Later in the expedition, seven men would ascend the shoulders of the volcano Mount Erebus to reach its smoking summit. But the real goal of the expedition was the South Pole itself.

The polar journey started without a hitch. The route south from Hut Point was already familiar to Shackleton. He had traversed 320 miles (515 km) of it out and then back again with Scott and Wilson in 1902, with Scott as the leader on the *Discovery* Expedition. This time, in 1908, Shackleton himself was in charge. If all went well, he would return from this a hero to the nation, redeemed in the eyes of all, especially his own.

One by one the ponies weakened and were shot and butchered. Their meat was cached, in supply depots along with other provisions, guaranteeing supplies for the journey home months later. On November 26 the explorers passed the southernmost point ever reached by man—82°17' S, where Scott's southern advance had turned back. The way forward now was entirely new. Whatever lay beyond was Shackleton's to discover.

He described the experience later in his book, *The Heart of the Antarctic*.

> "As the days wore on and mountain after mountain came into view, grimly majestic, the consciousness of our insignificance seemed to grow upon us. We were but tiny black specks crawling slowly across the white plain, and bending our puny strength to the task of wresting from nature secrets preserved inviolate through all the ages."

With every step new land came into view and mountain peaks bearing southeast came across their track; it was a range the men knew they would have to cross to reach their goal.

Going the distance

The distance covered so far had not been enough to meet the average required to make it to the Pole and back. One month and three hundred miles (482 km) out, they were already going on short rations to save as much as possible for the furthest south. On December 3, ascending a low peak that Shackleton named Mt. Hope, they first laid eyes on the great glacier that would be their highway south through the mountains and up to the high plateau they knew must be its source. He named this river of ice the Beardmore Glacier, in honor of one of the expedition's financial backers.

The last of the ponies, Socks, was lost down a crevasse near the glacier's base, and the four men hitched themselves to the thousand-pound weight of the pony sledges and began that most gruelling of polar tasks, man-hauling. Shackleton's book recounts the march—day after day of dragging the sledge uphill over hard blue ice riven by crevasses, their distances far short of the necessary average, and already going on short rations with hunger as their constant companion. But each day also had its reward—new land underfoot, continually opening ahead as they slowly advanced southwards, and thousands of feet upwards toward the plateau. As early as December 11, they imagined that plateau, and the head of the glacier, to be just a day or two's march farther along. Falls and injuries threatened success, and even survival, but there was nothing to be done but bandage the wounds and march along in pain and silence, hoping for the best. Shackleton confided their optimism in his diary on December 14: "To-night our hopes are high that we are nearly at the end of the rise and that soon we will reach our longed-for plateau. Then southward indeed! Food is the determining factor with us. We did 7½ miles (12 km) to-day."

Each day recorded a similar optimism, that the plateau was just ahead, and a similar mention of increasing hunger. "Hunger" to them was just a discomfort to be borne as a part of the work at hand, a minor price to pay for the honor and glory of discovery. No one really thought of it in real terms of the debilitation that was even now sapping their strength, and from which they would never recover on the reduced rations the four had all agreed to. They began leaving short rations in the depots, a dangerous tactic gambling on even greater daily distances on the return journey, and finding ways to "spin out" the food remaining for a greater distance outbound. In doing this, they kept the attainment of the Pole still within reach—barely. Having come so far, they were not about to give up.

Short commons

By December 20 they had reduced their breakfast to one pannikin of hoosh, and their lunch to three biscuits with a pannikin of cocoa. "To-day we did 11 miles 950 yards. (17 km) . . . Still we are getting on; we have only 279 miles (450 km) to go, and then we will have reached the Pole." At that rate it would take seven more weeks traveling to the Pole and back, clearly an impossible task, yet their optimism remained undiminished.

Christmas Day, the one day they had planned for a feast, in which they would allow themselves a full ration, loomed like a bright beacon ahead on these endless days of hard work. "We are very far away from all the world and home thoughts have been much with us to-day, thoughts interrupted by pitching forward into a hidden crevasse more than once. . . . We are all two degrees subnormal, but fit as can be. It is a fine open-air life and we are getting south." They could not, or would not, see how weakened they had become on the short rations, far from enough to sustain the high-altitude man-hauling that had become their daily round. On the following day, at an elevation of 9,500 feet (2,900 meters), they were on the plateau, and had finally lost sight of the nunatak mountain peaks behind them, the last vestiges of land to the north. "This shortness of food is unpleasant, but if we allow ourselves what, under ordinary circumstances, would be a reasonable amount, we would have to abandon all idea of getting far south."

Summit fever

It is one thing to make a plan and then commit all resources to its fulfilment. It is quite another to push beyond the physically possible in a futile attempt to achieve the impossible.

The term "summit fever" will be familiar to those who have followed the history of recent expeditions to the summit of Mt. Everest in Nepal. In two words it encapsulates the very broad notion of completion of a long-sought goal in the face of overwhelming obstacles, just below the summit of the mountain. That real geographical place represents for many the metaphysical summit of a life's ambition, an accomplishment available only to the few, and at great financial and personal expense.

After months of striving, weather conditions may preclude a summit attempt. The sheer numbers of people massed at that base camp, who must use a single trail to reach the peak and then return, may not all make it up and back during the very brief window of time that will be available. As some recent expeditions have shown, to do so is both foolhardy and, for some, deadly. But those who have chosen this goal, when they have reached the highest base camp before that elusive summit, often will not be denied their conquest.

Reading Shackleton's words in the comfort of our modern rooms, we can sympathize with the struggle he faced with his men as they slowly drew nearer to their goal. We can imagine the conversations they must have had beneath the fluttering canvas of their tent; thoughts and debates about the wisdom of pushing forward when they were at such extremes of hunger and deprivation. Whatever their private reservations may have been, their collective decision remained: "Push on!"

We can see, however, what they could not, or would not. They were already at the extreme limit of their physical human endurance, but the goal of their entire endeavor was so close. A few more days of this travail and they could turn for home and the accolades of an adoring nation, a place where their names would *forever* be in the history books. The foolhardiness of the plan that is so evident to us now, must have seemed to them but a gamble, a bargain at the price of only a few more days' hunger. "We are only 198 miles (318 km) off our goal now . . . We have only 150 lb. per man to pull, but it is more severe work that the 250 lb. per man up the glacier was," Shackleton wrote on December 29, adding in a classic understatement, "The Pole is hard to get." "Only 198 miles—almost four hundred out and back to *this* desolate point— four more weeks' man-hauling at the present rate of twelve miles (19 km) a day, with another thousand after that to the safety of the base camp."

Summit fever. New Year's Eve found them camped at 86° 54' S, with three weeks' food and two week's biscuits. They had yet to wake up to the fact that what they were asking of themselves was impossible. Had their intellects become so clouded that they did not recognize the folly of clinging to that hopeless goal? "Please God the weather will be fine the next fourteen days," he wrote two days later. "Then all will be well," as though having struggled this far; surely luck would see them through. And then "Tomorrow we must risk making a depot on the plateau, and make a dash for it, but even then, if this surface continues, we will be two weeks in carrying it through."

The reality of their situation finally caught up with them. Shackleton's words of January 4, 1909, must have been bitter indeed. "The end is in sight." They would have to give up the idea of reaching the Pole, and settle for some second-best result. "We can only go on for three more days at the most, for we are weakening rapidly." The hope was now to reach another, less significant coordinate on this vast and featureless plain. "We hope to reach within 100 geographical miles of the Pole; under the circumstances we can expect to do very little more."

"We have done our best"

After a three-day blizzard they left the sledges behind and made one more outward march to plant the flag at the furthest south ever reached by man to that date, 88°23'S. They were ninety-seven geographical miles (112 statute miles or 180 km) short of the South Pole. "There is only one thing that lightens the disappointment, and that is the feeling that we have done all we could. It is the forces of nature that have prevented us from going right through. I cannot write more."

Had that blizzard not stopped them in their tracks, they might have gone onward, most likely beyond the limit of their endurance. As it turned out, the four men barely made it home alive. That 750-mile (1,200 km) return journey is another tale of hardship and starvation, met with inspiring courage and endurance.

This can be taken as a cautionary tale to any who would test their own capacity to the limit beyond which safe recovery might be doubtful, if not impossible. It applies to more than physical endurance in extreme environments. The more dearly held the goal, the harder it is to give up. The immutable laws of nature, the character of human behavior, and the mathematics of profit and loss do not change simply because we hope that our best efforts will make them change.

Even though Shackleton never made it to the South Pole, no one can accuse him of giving up too soon, or "not going the distance." It was a goal that circumstance and hardship prevented him from ever achieving. The hundreds of miles of hard travel got him close, but for all his effort, still fell short. The additional hundreds of miles of the return trip, on short rations, nearly killed him and his companions. He wrote to his wife, "I thought you would rather have a live donkey than a dead lion." He gave it his all. As an inspiration to others, his work has left behind an immutable legacy.

Others, a few years later, completed that goal for him, again the result of great collective, but also great personal endeavor. In terms of geographical exploration, new goals were envisioned, and then achieved. Further exploration of Antarctica, the ongoing study of weather, glaciers and the oceans continues to this day, and increases the understanding of the world we live in. All this is built upon the foundation that Shackleton and others laid in the early 1900s—the ambition of a few men to do something that had yet to be done; to make a plan and reach a place that had always been just out of reach.

"Going the distance" is not a measure of having reached the goal, but of giving one's all in its pursuit. Shackleton fell short in his dream of reaching the South Pole, but is best remembered for having tried. He knew how to strive for big goals, and also knew when to turn back.

As each of us confronts our own limitations in the pursuit of goals, it is worthwhile to keep in mind these fundamental lessons gleaned from Shackleton's attempt. Firstly, it is our sense of the future, our ability to shape that future—collectively as well as individually—and our pursuit of long-range goals that define our humanity. Secondly, the shape of that future can be largely of our own choosing, working with what we have and striving for that which is just out of reach. Thirdly, it matters less whether we attain that goal, and more that we have seen a future that does not yet exist, have made a plan, have a goal, and then have done the best we can to attain it. Ultimately, the pursuit of a goal is as important as its attainment, perhaps even more so. Knowing when to turn around or when to pursue a different goal is tantamount to success, or even is success itself.

In looking at your own behavior, would you have had the wisdom to turn back, or would you have pushed yourself to the very end and risked everything?

Take one well known goal, sought by some today, for example. Time and again there are books, articles or movies about climbers on Everest who are so goal driven that they choose certain death to achieve their goal. This happened the very week we were editing this chapter[3] (June 2016) when three climbers continued towards the Everest summit despite being told that time had run out. None of them survived.

Shackleton's decision in 1909 was so remarkable because it reveals one of the most valuable lessons we can learn from the heroic age—when do we say, "It is time to turn back," and how do we convert abandoning a goal into an a positive outcome? Shackleton's brilliance was in seeking a memorable alternative achievement—going the distance to get within 100 geographical miles of the pole. Within that magical number—100—better, indeed, than they turned around at 103 geographical miles.

$$* * *$$

Sometimes in life, decisions are not clear; other times, as shown in the next chapter, they are abundantly clear, and one must take a monumental gamble.

---

[3] Article in the Guardian newspaper, June 6, 2016, http://gu.com/p/4kcnm/sbl
"*Subhash Paul, Paresh Nath and Goutam Ghosh continued towards summit despite advice time had run out,*" says Sherpa.

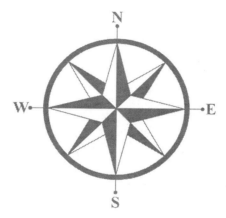

All Or Nothing: When Do You Take The Big Risk?

Sometimes you just have to plunge ahead.

What makes these stories of Antarctic exploration unforgettable? For many people it is that the early explorers, Scott, Shackleton, Amundsen, Mawson and their companions took such massive risks. Once the big decision was made, there was no turning back; it was all or nothing. They ventured out into the unknown with only the supplies they had the forethought to bring, with no hope of rescue should their plans fall into disaster. Frequently, it was a case of "do or die trying," often with the expedition leader at the front, with his own survival as much at risk as anyone else's.

Building upon the experiences of those who had gone before, they learned to anticipate many of the hazards. But not all of them. For all of the painstaking study and careful preparation seen in Chapter 4, each of the expeditions had to learn the painful lessons of discovery and exploration—extremes of cold and winds never before encountered, blizzards and whiteouts, marauding sea ice and yawning crevasses, and the encroaching weakness of vitamin deficiency.

Over time, these became less hazardous. The price of being first to see the uncharted shore or reach the long-sought goal was to be paid in discomfort and gruelling work, but not in lives. Once the Pole had been won, new and ever more dangerous goals seemed to loom over the horizon. Mawson stretched his teams across fifteen hundred miles over an unapproachable coastline; Shackleton envisioned a crossing of the continent.

Each new gamble was unique, the dangers were clear, the risks ever-present, and the outcome always uncertain. And on occasion deadly. Of the 165 men who set out to explore the Antarctic, eleven did not return. Listed on the page opposite, they were victims of the ravages of extended exposure, accident, and, for two of them, a failure to heed the clear patterns of the sea ice.

A higher fatality rate than that for ordinary occupations back at home perhaps, but this sort of adventuring attracts those with a desire for experiences that are out of the ordinary, for whom the added risk only adds spice to their everyday life. Considering the magnitude and variety of all the risks that all these explorers took, it is remarkable that so few died.

Each expedition relied on multiple, different, high-risk activities, all of which had to succeed as planned. Scott's *Discovery* Expedition in 1901-1904 involved much more than just penetrating the sea ice to find a good harbour on Antarctica in which to set up a scientific hut. This was to be an undertaking rife with unknown hazards. The preparations and planning were as complete as they could be given the men had precious little polar experience to bring to bear. Once their ship was frozen in for the winter, they would have no way out, and no one on whom to depend for relief but themselves.

In addition to the first manned balloon ascent and aerial photography in Antarctica, Scott's *Discovery* teams accomplished one of the first penetrations to the far south, and also went westward onto the Antarctic plateau, all with equipment that was entirely new to the men. Early forays into the adjacent territory showed how shockingly cold and dangerous the Antarctic could be for novices. One man, George Vince, lost his life coming home from what should have been a routine outing. Other teams came perilously close to death, barely surviving falls into crevasses and

Deaths on Expeditions

Expedition	Leader	# in Shore Parties	# of Deaths in Antarctica	Approximate Cause of Death
Discovery Expedition	Scott	46	1	*Accident:* Vince slipped on icy cliff.
Nimrod Expedition	Shackleton	15	0	
Terra Nova Expedition	Scott	31	5	*Accident:* Evans suspected head injury after a fall. *Exposure and want:* Scott, Bowers, Oates and Wilson of multiple causes including lack of food and oil. Died on their return from the South Pole.
Norwegian Anatarctic Expedition	Amundsen	9	0	
Australian Anatarctic Expedition	Mawson (Frank Wild for Queen Mary Land division)	26	2	*Accidents:* Ninnis fell in crevasse; Mertz died from accidental vitamin A poisoning after eating dog liver.
Endurance Expedition	Shackleton (Weddell Sea side)	28	0	
	Mackintosh (Ross Sea Party)	10	3	*Scurvy:* Spencer-Smith, after extended sledging. (Ross Sea Party) *Accident:* On ill-advised trek over sea ice from Hut Point to Cape Evans, Mackintosh and Hayward fell through the ice.
Total		**165**	**11**	

Assessment:
3 were due to unforseen accidental falls.
4 were the result of extended time in the field with insufficient nutrition available.
2 have since become avoidable, due to the discovery and understanding of vitamins.
2 were entirely avoidable, the result of setting forth on unstable sea ice.

bouts with scurvy. Their experiences, dearly paid, marked the hard-won beginning of a learning curve on which the second season's successes were built. Not without risk, of course, extending ever farther afield in the assured self-confidence of those who have faced the hardest conditions and prevailed.

Their adventures sparked the accolades of an admiring world, and a desire for more discoveries in this new and exciting continent. The unknown territory could be made known. The South Pole was now within reach. With only just a little more work, the facing of just a few more dangers, it could be won. Through some combination of trust, faith, luck, gut instinct and ingenuity, the vast majority of the men managed to survive. In all the higher risk scenarios described specifically in this chapter, not only did they survive—there was not even one occurrence of a serious injury or broken limb.[4]

The temptation grew to go just a little farther. Driven by ambition, the leaders of these expeditions decided, each for his own reasons, to take on a little more risk. Sometimes, it was much more than just a little. In the spirit of "nothing ventured, nothing gained," the men under their command agreed to go along.

Drawing the line

To an observer looking at the events over a hundred years after they occurred, one of the most terrifying risks that any heroic age Antarctic explorer actually took did not happen in Antarctica. It happened in New Zealand in 1910.

Before leaving England, Scott had purposefully changed the registration of the *Terra Nova,* to the Royal Yacht Squadron. This gambit enabled the ship to be exempt from the British maritime regulation dictating that a Plimsoll line (the mark on the ship's hull indicating the safe draft level) had to be painted on its side. At the time of the *Terra Nova's* sailing, this line had long been required by British maritime law, but would not become an international

---

[4] One of the most remarkable things about the heroic age of Antarctic exploration was how very tough and resilient these men were. There were frequent cases of frostbite, snow blindness, and scurvy from which the men reliably recovered. Of the few permanent injuries, Aeneas Mackintosh's loss of an eye while unloading the *Nimrod*, and Perce Blackborow's amputation of several toes while on Elephant Island, were the most severe.

standard until twenty years in the future.

The ship was heavily loaded at Cardiff and the line would certainly have been below the water level. Although there was considerable risk in sailing the ship in this condition, the journey to New Zealand would pass through calmer seas. While the *Terra Nova* was docked in New Zealand late in 1910, the ship went through final preparations for the voyage to Antarctica. Many extra supplies, including more men and their gear, were added to the ship for the journey south. Also included were tons more coal, more scientific equipment, all the dogs and ponies, three motor sledges and their spare parts, and tons more food and other supplies. The decks of the ship were laden with cargo, coal in sacks, oil in tins, and three huge containers holding the motor sledges.

Everyone boarding the *Terra Nova* knew she was perilously low in the water, but they all took the risk to sail from New Zealand to Antarctica across some of the most treacherous and stormy seas in the world. Would *you* have dared say, "This is not for me?"

Two days out of port, the *Terra Nova* hit a storm. The gale lasted for thirty-six intense hours, during which the ship began to fill with water. The pumps, clogged by balls of oil and coal, refused to draw. It looked to everyone aboard that she was going to sink. As she settled lower in the water, the men working in shifts kept her barely afloat by bailing until the pumps could be restored. The *Terra Nova* survived thanks to the hard work of these men. Had she gone down, the expedition would never have been heard from again. Two of the dogs were washed overboard, and two of the ponies died in their stalls, but in the end the storm passed on, and the ship resumed her passage to Antarctica.

It is truly remarkable that they survived on such a heavily-laden ship in such a fierce storm. It is even more remarkable that Scott and his men went on the ship in the first place—that they did not consider making the necessary trade-offs between the scientific pursuits of the expedition (men and scientific instruments), the polar ambitions (motor sledges, dogs and ponies) and all the other food and supplies they thought were needed for success on all counts.

They risked it all in pursuit of their ambitions, and they survived thanks to their tenacity and hard work throughout the entire storm.

Were they brave or foolhardy, or a bit of both? Certainly they were tested.

Barrier Ice or land: which would you choose?

Scott was not the only big risk taker. All the expedition leaders took massive, "throw the dice," risks in achieving their goals. Exactly one-and-a-half months after the *Terra Nova* hit the storm at sea, Amundsen docked the *Fram* in the Bay of Whales. His intention was to build his base, Framheim, on the Barrier Ice near this bay. This location had the advantage of being sixty miles (96 km) closer to the South Pole than McMurdo Sound where Scott was building his Cape Evans Hut.

There was one big difference. Scott was building his Cape Evans Hut on solid land; Amundsen's Framheim would be built on the floating ice of the Barrier, which even then was known to break away into icebergs or disintegrate into smaller pieces.

The region where Framheim was built has an interesting history linked to Scott and Shackleton. It was here in 1902 that Scott and his men had launched a hydrogen-filled army reconnaissance balloon to make the first aerial ascent in Antarctica, at an inlet into the Barrier they named Balloon Bight. Scott made the first ascent and Shackleton the second, but then the wind increased making Reginald Skelton's ascent dangerous. Skelton was chief engineer and the *Discovery* Expedition photographer.

Shackleton's ship, the *Nimrod*, returned to the area in 1908, but could not find Balloon Bight. The Barrier Ice around this bay had broken away, leaving in its place a completely different inlet they named the Bay of Whales for the hundreds of whales in the area. This was all the proof Shackleton needed: no matter how permanent the Barrier Ice might look, it was unstable.

Amundsen had a different view. He had studied the scant history of the area and had decided that parts of the Bay of Whales ice shelf were stable enough to build on because they were grounded. Since his sole ambition was to be first to the Pole, he decided that the advantage of being sixty miles (96 km) closer was worth the risk. Amundsen's approach entailed an additional sizeable challenge—due to their starting position from the Bay of Whales, he and his team would have to pioneer an entirely new route to the South Pole; they would not be going over ground that Scott and Shackleton had covered on previous expeditions.

Amundsen took a major risk in setting up his base on the ice. Had the Barrier Ice broken in the coming year, his hut, Framheim and everyone there would have been lost to the sea. The entire tale of the discovery of the South Pole would be different, and Amundsen would be remembered as a daring risk taker and an unlucky decision maker. Of course, had the *Terra Nova* actually sunk, as it came so dreadfully near to doing, the same might have been thought of Scott.

One can debate who took the bigger risk. Each leader had his own skills, made his own decisions, and decided which risks were acceptable. In some aspects of polar travel, though, Amundsen planned better and therefore took fewer risks. For example, his depots were closer together than Scott's and better sign-posted, but there is no denying that setting Framheim on the ice was an enormous risk that in the end paid off handsomely.

Given the shorter mileage to the pole, and fewer days travelling on the colder and windier polar plateau at ten thousand feet (3,000 m) above sea level, their overall journey was less physically debilitating. More of their trek was spent in the slightly milder environment of the sea-level Barrier. Framheim and all of Amundsen's men survived the "Barrier Ice" gamble, and Amundsen achieved his goal of being first to the pole.

Two hundred miles and six weeks away from base camp

Imagine you are due to fly somewhere today. Will you check your flight status online? If so, why? To make sure your flight is on time?

To make sure weather conditions or mechanical failures are not going to result in a cancelled flight? Like many people, we rely on this information for reassurance.

Now imagine it is over one hundred years ago, when there was no communication or information to be had. You were totally dependent upon a returning ship for your safety, but you had no way of knowing if it actually could reach you. It might arrive, but there was a very real possibility it might not. It was expected that if, for whatever reason, the ship could not return, you and your men would have to fend for yourselves. Would you have volunteered for that?

Six men did, as part of Scott's *Terra Nova* Expedition. They were a small team planning to explore a new area of Antarctica hundreds of miles from base. Their original plan, in 1911, was to explore a region called King Edward VII Land, located to the east, near the Bay of Whales. Finding Amundsen already encamped there, they accepted his offer of Antarctic hospitality and enjoyed a cordial visit, but declined his invitation to also be based there, opting instead to explore a different location. They chose Victoria Land, lying west of the Ross Sea.

The small team became known as the Northern Party. They successfully wintered over near Cape Adare, but due to the geography of the location were unable to carry out much exploration. When the *Terra Nova* successfully returned as planned to pick them up in early January 1912 (the Antarctic summer), the Northern Party decided to be dropped off farther south on the coast, near Evans Cove, to investigate this previously unexplored region of the Antarctic. This new location was closer, but still two hundred miles (320 km) north of Scott's main base at Cape Evans.

The new plan was simple enough. The six-man Northern Party—Campbell, Priestley, Levick, Abbott, Browning, and Dickason—would conduct scientific and geological analysis in the area of Evans Cove, and the *Terra Nova* would pick them up in a pre-assigned location six weeks later. As with all the early expeditions, they had no way of contacting the ship, and the ship had no way of contacting them. The risks to ships in Antarctica were many—they could catch fire, sink in a storm, hit an iceberg, or get crushed in the ice pack. Imagine how isolating it would be, waiting for a ship to pick you up, all the time wondering if one of these calamities had happened.

Landing six men in Evans Cove with only six weeks of supplies and a clear expectation that they would be picked up six weeks later was a calculated risk, but a large one all the same. At Evans Cove, the exploration aims were better met. However, when the six weeks were up, the ship could not retrieve them. The sea had frozen over and the ship could not get anywhere near them. The *Terra Nova*, herself in danger of being frozen in for the winter, had to continue north and leave the men to fend for themselves. One can only imagine what the Northern Party team members felt, waiting ashore with their very limited equipment, clothing and food, ultimately realizing the ship would not be able to pick them up.

With winter coming on, they set up camp at a place they named Inexpressible Island. Their tents were not sufficient protection from the brutal Antarctic winter, so they dug a cave into the ice to make their home. Small though it was, twelve feet by nine feet, they maintained the naval custom of "partitioning" to make a "wardroom" for the three officers, and a "mess deck" for the men. The ice cave was so cramped, the two groups could always hear each other's voices, but in the unwritten tradition of the sea, they chose to ignore the words. They survived the winter in this dark, ultimately squalid hovel in the ice, to emerge months later prepared to save themselves.

For them, the next big risk arrived once spring came. They could either wait for rescue, or make a treacherous coastal traverse to Cape Evans. Though weakened by lack of food and sunlight, and suffering from frostbite and intestinal ailments, they took matters into their own hands and decided to hike. Thankfully they all survived. Later in the year, the *Terra Nova* was able to make it back to both Cape Adare and Evans Cove to retrieve the geological specimens they had left behind.

Next time you are checking your flight status online or looking at the departure boards at the airport, spend a minute thinking what it must have been like being part of Scott's Northern Party. Would you have been willing to be dropped off at a point on the Antarctic coast with only six weeks' worth of supplies, with the understanding that the ship would return to collect you (hopefully) in six weeks, and knowing there was no way of contacting you if something happened?

Fifteen hundred miles and one year away from base camp

Fortunately for Scott's Northern Party, they were *only* two hundred miles (320 km) from base and were able to trek back to Cape Evans even in their weakened state. If you thought that was risky, imagine setting up camp fifteen hundred miles (2,400 km) away from base.

At roughly the same time as the Northern Party's travails, Mawson's Australian Antarctic Expedition (1911-1914) was underway. His aim was to explore a two-thousand-mile strip of Antarctic coast. A common ambition of all the expeditions was to explore new territory, in many cases claiming the new land for their country. Mawson's plan was to set up a base at Cape Denison, with a secondary party of eight men, led by Frank Wild, to be dropped off fifteen hundred miles farther east on an ice shelf adjoining Queen Mary Land. (A third party was left at another location.) The intention was that Wild and his men would explore the coast, and one year later the *Aurora* would return to pick them up.

One of the challenges Wild and his men encountered was discovering how severely Queen Mary Land was beset with strong winds, which hampered their work. The winds were actually even stronger in Mawson's base at Cape Denison, where they were near-constant hurricane force.

Unlike the other expeditions of the era, Mawson and Wild had some rudimentary early radio communication equipment. The intention was that Cape Denison would at least be able to receive some Morse code radio communication from Wild and his team. However, the strong winds destroyed Wild's radio mast and

Mawson's team at Cape Denison were unable to erect their mast to its full height, thus limiting its range. Despite the advantages of technology, as well as excellent planning and preparation, Wild and his team were as cut off from all communication with their ship and companions as any previous expeditions had been.

They had supplies, but only enough to last for the duration of their planned stay. If the ship could not return, they would have been even more severely challenged than the Northern Party by a dangerous shortage of food and fuel. While they would have been more comfortable in their hut than Campbell's and Priestley's Northern Party were in their ice cave, the distance and difficult terrain between the two sites meant that Wild and his men could never have survived the long journey overland back to Cape Denison. Fortunately, the *Aurora* successfully returned to pick them up on time.

This is another example of a big risk that paid off with everyone surviving. Even if you would have taken the six-week, two-hundred-mile drop-off, would you have taken the bigger risk of a one year, fifteen-hundred-mile drop-off?

"These are men!" [5]

The last "all or nothing" risk to consider is one of the most famous in the history of exploration. In Chapter 3 we saw how Shackleton

---

[5] Worsley, Frank; Shackleton's Boat Journey, p. 216. "In the evening the manager [of the Stromness Whaling Station] told Sir Ernest that a number of old captains and sailors wished to speak to and shake hands with him and us [Worsley and Crean]. We went into a large, low room, full of captains and mates and sailors, and hazy with tobacco smoke. Three or four white-haired veterans of the sea came forward; one spoke in Norse and the manager translated. He said that he had been at sea over forty years; that he knew this stormy Southern Ocean intimately, from South Georgia to Cape Horn, from Elephant Island to the South Orkneys, and that never had he heard of such a wonderful feat of daring seamanship as bringing the twenty-two foot open boat from Elephant Island to South Georgia, and then to crown it, tramping across the snow and rocky heights of the interior, and that he felt it an honour to meet and shake hands with Sir Ernest and his comrades. He finished with a dramatic gesture:

"'These are men!'

"All the seamen present then came forward and solemnly shook hands with us in turn."

skillfully reframed the goal of his Imperial Trans-Antarctic Expedition from being the first to walk from one side of Antarctica to the other, to one of bringing all of the twenty-eight men from the *Endurance* home alive after the ship was crushed by the ice. In Chapter 6 we saw how Frank Wild maintained order and hope when he and twenty-one other men from the *Endurance* were left on Elephant Island awaiting rescue.

Now we come to the next and final section of that story. After the ice floes they were camped upon broke up, Shackleton and his men spent six days traveling in the three *Endurance* lifeboats, some nights camping on ice floes, until that was deemed too dangerous. With a great deal of difficulty, a tremendous amount of skill, and a bit of luck, they successfully navigated the icy waters and landed—frozen, exhausted and starving—on a small uninhabited island called Elephant Island. Named for the huge seals that live there, this rocky island was far from the path of any whaler or other ship.

Shackleton and Worsley determined the only practicable plan for rescue was to sail the largest of the lifeboats to the whaling stations at South Georgia. It was a plan born of desperation. The likelihood of its success was small, but the consequences of failure to summon help were enormous. No one in the world knew that the *Endurance* had been shattered, that they were now stranded on this desolate shore. No one would come looking for them. Far from any shipping channel, they likely would not be found before all had succumbed to starvation.

They would sail in the *James Caird*. Henry "Chips" McNish, the highly skilled ship's carpenter, had previously built up the sides and reinforced the keel of the *James Caird* using wood from the wrecked *Endurance*. He caulked the seams between the wooden planks of the boat with lamp wick, and then sealed them with the expedition artist's oil paints, and decked her over with Venesta plywood and canvas. But the *James Caird* was only twenty-two-and-a-half-feet long; South Georgia was eight hundred miles (1300 km) away across the most treacherous seas in the world. Waves could easily be forty- to fifty- feet high and rogue waves caused by heavy storms and winds could be much higher.

The boat's crew would consist of Shackleton, Worsley, Crean, McNish, McCarthy and Vincent. Against the advice of some of his men, Shackleton insisted that the *James Caird* be heavily loaded with ballast to keep it low in the water. Even with all these preparations, it remained a *very* small vessel sailing in very rough seas, manned by men who had already been weakened by exposure and poor rations from their experience of already spending more than 187 days on the ice.

One could argue that at almost every juncture of the *James Caird* sea journey, the six men encountered bad luck. When they were launching the *James Caird*, the swell increased and many of the men got soaked to the waist. Then she almost capsized near the shore and also came close to smashing into the rocks. Vincent and McNish ended up getting thrown into the water. With no change of clothing, it was unlikely any of them would dry out for days, or possibly for the entire two-week journey.

The list of serious challenges they encountered during their voyage was nearly endless: very rough seas that often nearly swamped the boat; reindeer sleeping bags that moulted and shed fur continuously, clogging the pump and getting into their food; and constantly damp and always uncomfortable clothing. One of their two barrels of drinking water became contaminated with salt water, so that by the end of the journey they were constantly and dangerously thirsty. Ice continually formed on the surfaces of the boat, requiring them to go out on the slippery deck in rough seas to chip it away. The boat was incredibly small and horribly uncomfortable for six men, and the pitching of the boat and the rock ballast denied them sleep.

They hit gale force winds and storms and encountered such constantly cloudy skies that during the whole voyage, Worsley was only able to take four navigational sun sightings to confirm their course to South Georgia. On the eleventh day of the journey, Shackleton thought he saw a break in the weather, revealing some clear skies. What he was actually seeing was the crest of a rogue wave, so high above them that Shackleton in all his years at sea had never seen a wave so large. For a terrifying minute, it seemed that the *James Caird* must certainly break up or be swamped, and they would surely all die. Remarkably, the boat and the men survived.

Once they did eventually reach South Georgia, they were kept offshore another day-and-a-half by a raging hurricane, before finally landing in the isolated shelter of King Haakon Bay on the *wrong* side of South Georgia. The only inhabited sections of the island were the whaling stations on the opposite side. Given the perilous sea journey they had just completed, the only way to reach one of them was overland, across the uncharted, unexplored mountains and glaciers of the interior.

After several days' rest, they decided on a course of action. With McNish and Vincent too weak to make the journey, Shackleton left McCarthy to look after them. The plan was that Shackleton, Crean and Worsley would hike across the mountains to the Stromness whaling station. They had no sleeping bag or tent, no climbing equipment except a length of alpine rope. For an ice axe they had only the carpenter's adze, for crampons only the screws he had driven through the welts of their boots. Their map was a chart of the island's coast, with no details at all of the mountainous interior. With only a limited amount of food and enough oil in their one Primus to last two days, this was yet another awe-inspiring polar decision to *do or die trying.*

No one had ever done this journey before, even with adequate climbing equipment. The distance to go was not great (they estimated about twenty miles or 32 km), but they knew the way would be blocked by mountains reaching possibly as high as six thousand feet, laced with glaciers and sudden drops. The journey was uncharted, the mountain passes unknown, and the Antarctic winter was about to begin.

After several attempts to find a way up and down through the mountains, the three men reached a point where they had to make a desperate decision. They were getting weaker and could no longer afford the energy to backtrack once again to find a route through. They were at the top of a mountain pass and decided the only way down was to use the coil of rope like a toboggan and, with one man sitting behind another, slide down the mountain. They had no idea what lay at the bottom. If it was a snow bank, they would probably survive. If rocks or ice, they would be killed or severely injured; in this environment, it amounted to the same thing.

In a very rare instance of real good luck, it was snow—and they survived their exhilarating slide down the mountain. The three men continued hiking but could not stop to sleep. With no shelter or sleeping bags, sleeping on the bare snow in the mountains could easily result in death from exposure. At one point Shackleton let the other two men take a short nap. He woke them after five minutes, telling them that they had slept for half an hour. They eventually descended out of the mountains into the whaling station. They had hiked almost non-stop for more than thirty-six hours.

The whalers sent out a boat and quickly rescued McCarthy, McNish and Vincent, and recovered the *James Caird*. Shackleton's new quest was now to reach the twenty-two men still marooned on Elephant Island. Two great obstacles lay in his path—the sea ice, and the Great War then raging, limiting the availability of ships. It took Shackleton four attempts on four different ships before he reached Elephant Island on the Chilean steam tug *Yelcho*. Thanks to Frank Wild's leadership, Shackleton found all twenty-two men alive—128 days after leaving them behind and embarking on the *James Caird*.

In 2013, the modern explorer Tim Jarvis and his team built an exact replica of the *James Caird* and re-enacted Shackleton's boat journey using period clothing, food and navigational equipment. They suffered the same privations, faced the same hazards, and proved just how dreadful was Shackleton's boat journey, and how heroic was the overland crossing of South Georgia to reach the whaling station.

Shackleton's boat journey was a massive roll of the dice; the dangers were tremendous. But they never gave up believing they would survive. Despite all the bad luck, they *never* gave in. They never said, "We can't do this." They believed they could do the impossible, and they actually did.

When you've taken the big risk and bad luck hits, what do *you* do? Shackleton, Crean and Worsley's story resonates with so many people around the world for the very reason that we all encounter bouts of bad luck, but Shackleton and his men proved that teamwork, sheer grit and determination, and self-reliance can pull you through just about anything. The trick is to never, ever give up trying.

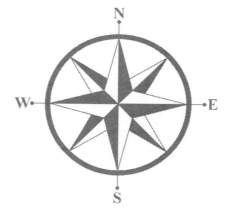

What Is Your Higher Purpose?

Why go?

The question posed in the title of this chapter, *"What Is Your Higher Purpose?"* is not an idle one. By its very title this chapter seems to want to dignify every action. But not every human endeavor has a higher purpose, nor does it need one. There is nothing specifically ennobling in just having breakfast, or taking the dog for a walk. The vast majority of everyday events, or even momentous ones, are just intrinsic responses to a pressing local need.

The matter becomes a little more complicated when today's activities and decisions set in motion a course of consequences unfolding over time, or affecting others. Business and social planning inevitably have a broader reach. The commitment extends into the future, with a shared sense of obligation. Even when such planning involves larger contracts and many people, its fulfilment is a matter of business ethics and common respect for others. It need not be guided by a lofty sense of principle.

Why did these Antarctic explorers take on such monumental tasks, at such enormous risk and personal privation? Certainly there was little enough financial reward in it. Even after they returned home with geographic and scientific discoveries, the expedition leaders and others spent years lecturing, writing books and fundraising to pay the debts of the past expedition or fund the next one. There must have been something more to their drive.

This notion of "something more" is borne out time and again in the men's diaries and reminiscences about their experiences in the Antarctic. A few very basic words, spoken by the seaman Tom Crean, reveal one truth: "It is all for the good of science." Science—the sum total of all human investigation into the not-yet-known, a pyramid ever-growing with the addition of each new unrecorded bit of data—was one of the guiding lights of polar expeditions during the heroic age. The other was geographical discovery. As long as there was an uncharted shore, or an unvisited place, the lure of that unknown pulled countless men into the harrowing extremes of the Poles, and sometimes did not release them.

Heroic era

Our stories come from the heroic era of Antarctic exploration, beginning with Scott's 1901 *Discovery* Expedition. Even a casual reading of first-hand accounts written during those expeditions will prove that the term "heroic" is fitting. There is an abundance of tales of stoic endurance in the face of appalling hardship, to fulfil what today may seem to be quixotic goals. During Shackleton's 1907-1909 *Nimrod* Expedition described in Chapter 10, he and three men reached their absolute limit and knew they had to turn back from their quest to the Pole, yet they pushed onward a few more miles south. Their main goal—that of being first to the Pole—was out of reach, but Shackleton wanted to be certain he had come within one hundred miles of the place. They may have been geographical miles which are somewhat longer than the more conventional statute miles, but just those few more miles even with the term *geographical* in front of it, somehow made his achievement in 1909 a little more worthy to him.

Other examples include Edward Wilson's source of strength and solace—"All will be as it is meant to be"—in a slim volume of poetry he brought on Scott's south polar journey in 1912, from which he never returned. Charlie Green, the cook on board the doomed *Endurance*, cooked one last dinner for the men as the ship was in her final stages of being crushed by the ice. That last meal was eaten on board in silence, an important final ritual. At the same time, the Ross Sea Party (see Chapter 8) on the far side of Antarctica, cobbled together food and materials, and at great personal risk and sacrifice laid depots from the Ross Sea to the Beardmore Glacier, rather than renege on a promise made to Shackleton.

There are too many similar examples to give them all scope in this chapter, but they were all the result of a conscious decision to press on, despite devastating hardship, in pursuit of an ephemeral goal that had more to do with the human spirit than with tangible reward. They all speak to the notion of a "higher purpose"—the idea that a driving force greater than sheer necessity can call forth reserves of energy untapped by everyday existence. Words like "duty" and "integrity" come to mind, but fail to capture the essence of "higher purpose."

Science versus discovery

Douglas Mawson took part in the *Nimrod* Expedition to try to determine the precise location of the South Magnetic Pole. On October 6, 1908, Mawson, Edgeworth David, and Alistair Mackay left the relative comfort of Shackleton's Cape Royds Hut for a 1,260-mile roundtrip across Antarctica. These three men were scientists first; explorers second. When they set out on their long journey heading west, then up and across the lofty plateau, geographical discovery was only one of their goals. Their main objective was to locate the one place in the entire Southern Hemisphere where their magnetic dip needle pointed down in a vertical line. There are only two places on Earth where this can happen—the North, and the South, Magnetic Poles.

By careful measurement, they came to that place on January 16, 1909, three months out from the hut at Cape Royds. They marked it on the chart, and noted the coordinates: 72°25' S, 155°16' E. Other than this positive identification of this dip needle, there was absolutely nothing to identify the Pole. It had no greater value than a confirmation of the elevation and appearance of 0° where all meridians converge onto a single point, a mathematical place on the globe, and that was all. Yet this was enough. Having determined the place, the three men turned for home, a cold and cheerless 630-mile slog down glaciers and across sea ice.

On that day, eight hundred miles (1,300 km) to the south, their expedition mates Ernest Shackleton, Jameson Adams, Eric Marshall, and Frank Wild were camped on another piece of this enormous featureless plateau, in their quest for that other Pole, that abstract place of 90° S. Their goal was not just to locate it, but to be the *first* men to do so, to "bag" the South Pole and claim it for Great Britain. They had come near enough to know it would be just another point on the empty plain of ice. It would not be reached this time.

Both parties would have a long struggle to get back to Cape Royds before the *Nimrod*, waiting offshore to relieve them and carry them home, would have to depart. Shackleton's goal was vindication after his previous failure to reach the Pole; Mawson's, to add one more invaluable piece to the growing pyramid of geo-magnetic science. Although their struggles were similar, their real successes were not. Whose name is better remembered today?

Three penguin eggs

Two years later, on Scott's *Terra Nova* Expedition, Edward Wilson, Birdie Bowers, and Apsley Cherry-Garrard set out on a winter journey from the hut at Cape Evans to collect recently laid eggs of the emperor penguin. These penguins were suspected to have chosen the dead of the Antarctic winter for their egg laying season. To retrieve the early embryo eggs for biological analysis, someone would have to leave the security of the hut and man-haul overland to the breeding colony in the darkest, coldest, most dangerous month of the year—July.

The plan was drawn up by Dr. Edward Wilson—an ornithologist as well as the expedition's physician and artist—who had long wanted to secure some fresh-laid eggs from this peculiar creature. A prevailing scientific idea at the time was that these primitive birds were closely related to the reptilian family, and that a close look at the embryo in the egg would demonstrate proof of Darwin's Theory of Evolution linking reptilian dinosaurs to birds. Wilson's goal—to bring home to the hut a clutch of emperor penguin eggs for further study—this was the object of the excursion, later to be known as "the worst journey in the world."

Cape Crozier lay a *mere* sixty-five miles (105 km) away, across a shelf of level frozen ice. Even in the heart of the Antarctic winter, he believed it should be manageable. Collecting the eggs and proving the link would be a massive scientific achievement.

Wilson selected his two companions in the comfort of the hut, long before anyone had an idea of the severe hardships to come. Cherry-Garrard and Bowers, for their part, agreed to go along and do their best. Their success, and indeed their survival, depended on Wilson's judgment in choosing just the right men for this work.

Taking the long view from the twenty-first century, it is clear to us that these men were woefully unprepared for the terrors that were soon to confront them. They set out in midwinter—on June 27, just after the winter solstice when the sun was at its farthest, and the "day" was a scant brightening of the dark sky. The temperatures would drop to fearsome depths, as they very soon discovered.

The Antarctic winter temperatures could dip as low as -77°F (-60.5°C). It was cold enough to freeze their clothing into rigid boards, and to chill the oil in their Primus stove to a viscous, unlightable gel. It was so intensely cold, that each night they used their body heat to thaw a way into their sleeping bags. They shivered so violently at night, their teeth cracked and they thought their bones would shatter. They found, on arising from the dismal comfort of their moulting reindeer-skin sleeping bags, that their clothing froze around them *instantly*. Remarkably, a temperature of -50°F would soon feel almost balmy to them.

After two-and-a-half weeks of this, they reached Cape Crozier and erected a modest stone shelter, roofed it over with their sledge and a floorcloth, and set out in search of the eggs. The way down to the sea ice that was home to the breeding colony of emperors was hard to find, and once found, nearly impossible to navigate in the dark days and nights. After a few days of concentrated effort, they managed to bring up three intact eggs, and a few birds to butcher for their skins and blubber.

Safe in their stone and cloth shelter, they wormed their way into the frozen bags and tried to go to sleep, but worse was yet to come. A blizzard wind, howling up the gravel slope, sucked at the canvas roof with ever greater fury, until with a great crack, it shredded itself into ribbons, and the three hapless campers were buried under an ever-deepening layer of snow. Hours later, as the gale began to ease, they discovered an even greater disaster. Their one tent, set up to protect some of their gear left outside the stone shelter, had been blown away. By now, they feared, it must be halfway to New Zealand.

In the dim twilight of the Antarctic morning they began to piece together the remnants of their gear and to try to figure out a way to get home alive. Here, luck favored these three. The tent had come to rest a few hundred yards away. Except for the tattered floorcloth, most of their gear remained intact, but they had barely enough food and fuel to make it back to Cape Evans.

The three of them worked as a team throughout the ordeal and never lost hope, drawing strength from one another and the intangible value of a shared belief that their greater purpose of this scientific endeavor outweighed any hardships they encountered. With their three eggs and their humanity still intact, they set off on foot for home, sixty-five icy miles (105 km) away. Not only did the three survive this "worst journey in the world" (the title of Cherry-Garrard's famous book), they preserved their humanity and self-respect throughout. In Cherry-Garrard's words, "We did not forget the *Please* and *Thank you*, which means much in such circumstances and all the little links with decent civilization which we could still keep . . ."

The eggs eventually made it to the Natural History Museum in London, where they were peremptorily examined and a paper was published. They were put into storage, and remain there to this day. Ironically, the embryos inside failed to deliver the evidence that Wilson had been seeking, to provide the evolutionary links between dinosaurs and birds.

But, in the end, the great significance of this effort was not about the eggs. It was about the man who conceived this audacious plan and the two who agreed to join him, not so much for the eggs or the science, but to see if it could be done. They proved that it could.

Four months later, these three set out on another such journey, partly for discovery and science, but just as much to prove that through careful planning and perseverance we can accomplish whatever we set out to do. Two of the three, Wilson and Bowers, did not survive that second journey, and perished in March 1912 on the way home from the South Pole. Their letters home from that last camp, described in Chapter 3, speak volumes towards our understanding of that higher purpose.

There is a remarkable footnote to the winter journey—the emperor penguin skins that Wilson, Bowers and Cherry-Garrard collected in 1911 were used as the control specimens in the 1960s studies to determine the change in DDT levels in Antarctic penguins. Without those skins, it would have been harder to prove the rapid rise of DDT in the world's environment. The benefits of their bold, hazardous expedition would live long beyond their own lives. DDT was banned in the United States in 1972 and in most countries in the 1980s.

A difficult choice: the living or the dead?

Sometimes two seemingly high purposes come into conflict, and one must be chosen above the other. This is exactly what happened on Scott's *Terra Nova* Expedition to the men who had chosen to stay over for that second winter in 1912. They faced an agonized atmosphere of bereavement and doubt. The failure of Scott's five-man Polar Party to return before winter closed in for good was certain proof that Scott and his men all died either getting to the Pole or on the long journey back. The fate of the Northern Party, six men who had been dropped off there by the *Terra Nova* in February 1912 to explore the area around Evans Cove for six weeks, was still unknown.

As described in Chapter 11, the plan had been for the *Terra Nova* to pick up the Northern Party on her voyage to Cape Evans later that year to relieve the shore party there. However, pack ice had kept the ship from reaching the Evans Cove shore at any of the proposed pickup or message posts. The team of six had been left to their fates, to survive or not on their own mettle, and then make their own way down the coast of Victoria Land to the base camp at Cape Evans.

That winter the shore party's leader, Dr. Edward Atkinson, and the twelve other men remaining at Cape Evans, had to decide which of the two important missions they would embark upon in the spring. Should they go overland to the aid of the Northern Party (who might or might not be alive), stranded on some inhospitable shore, exhausted and in dire need of help? Or, go south instead, looking for some sign of Scott and his men, who were *most assuredly* dead.

Atkinson assembled the men around the wardroom table in the dead of winter. Each man was allowed to speak his mind, and back up his decision with his own assessment of the situation, making his own call in the matter. And each man so doing would have to live with the results of his judgment, one way or the other.

Their choices were: to honor the dead, by searching for Scott and his men's remains; to seek among their effects the proof that they had reached the South Pole; or, attempt the rescue of the Northern Party who may or may not be still alive. Was proof of the attainment of the Pole by men now dead more valuable and more potent, than the relief of those who at least *might* be still among the living?

The final vote among those thirteen men at Cape Evans was to go south in search of the lost Polar Party. From our comfortable position here a century later, it is easy to criticize that decision—are not the living of infinitely more value than the dead?

But we are not those people. In their world, the concepts of honor and duty held great weight. As for the living, in the nature of this heroic age of Antarctic exploration, they had been entrusted with the responsibility to manage their own affairs, come what may. The Northern Party may have undergone great hardship over their unexpected second winter in the field, but these men could surely hold their own.

In the end, all six of the men of the Northern Party (Campbell, Priestley, Levick, Abbott, Browning, and Dickason) made it back to Cape Evans, which was one of the most incredible stories ever told about survival against extreme circumstances. And the search party that headed south did indeed find their lost captain and two of his companions, with the invaluable records of proof of their accomplished mission.

How important was it to find Scott's legacy over searching for possible living men? On the long and difficult journey back, Scott and his men had stopped to collect fossils, and used some of the last of their strength to carry them forward. Those fossils eventually helped to establish the geological theory of plate tectonics. Their journey, recorded in their written words, in Scott's photographs and Wilson's detailed drawings, helped define the structure of the Polar Plateau. Their final writings (described in Chapter 3) touched the soul of Britain for generations to come.

Had you been charged with the decision—rescue the living or vindicate the dead—what would you have done?

Without exception, every single person the authors have spoken to about this story has said that they would try to rescue the living. We, of course, would do the same—rescue the living. How interesting that a hundred years ago, the answer was so different. Without their discovery of Scott's, Wilson's and Bowers' tent, an amazing story of adventure and exploration would never have been told.

How high the purpose?

What if the higher purpose does little to illuminate the ennobling reach of the human spirit? What if instead of suffering and science, it serves personal ambition?

Ambition is not a bad thing. It is one of the innumerable traits that have driven the evolution of our society. Without it there would have been no monarchies or revolutions, no technological or medical advances, and no voyages of exploration and discovery.

Throughout the eighteenth and nineteenth centuries, the maritime nations of Europe sent their fleets out, often at great risk, to extend the limits of the known world. These missions expanded the reach of commerce and created wealth across developing markets. Fortune and its consort, fame, are two of the most seductive prospects of human endeavor. It comes as no surprise that many of us are motivated to action by their allure.

Roald Amundsen was no exception. He made his name in polar exploration during the *Belgica* Expedition 1897-1899, which was the first to over-winter in the Antarctic, and again in 1903 when his sloop the *Gjøa* became the first vessel to complete the fabled Northwest Passage. On his return to Norway, Amundsen was justly celebrated; his reputation as an explorer was settled. What could be next?

At the very beginning of 1909, it was believed that the North Pole had yet to be discovered, as neither Dr. Frederick Cook (who had years before been on the *Belgica* Expedition with Amundsen) nor Robert Peary had returned from their expeditions to announce their competing claims of attainment.

Amundsen saw this as an opportunity. He had already proven that careful preparation, the right ship, and the best handpicked men could accomplish what whole navies could not. He secured the exploration ship the *Fram* and outfitted her for the journey through and over the sea ice to the North Pole.

His plans were forestalled later in September 1909 by the publication of Dr. Frederick Cook's claim he had reached it in 1908

(Cook had a long and challenging return to civilization) and Robert Peary's claim he was first there in April 1909. Who was first can still be debated today. Here again, many men had struggled, and some perished, in fruitless efforts to attain that elusive end.

Having been conquered, the North Pole had lost its allure for Amundsen. The South Pole was still available for conquest, but not for long. Robert Scott was already heading south in the *Terra Nova* to claim that prize for himself.

Amundsen changed his plans. The *Fram* was already loaded with dogs and supplies for an assault on the Pole. Any Pole. Without notifying the owner of the ship, or even the men who had set sail on her, he decided to head secretly for Antarctica, intending to set up a base at the eastern end of the Great Ice Barrier. That location should provide a level route over the Barrier to a yet undiscovered glacier up through the mountains of South Victoria Land to the Polar Plateau and then to the Pole itself. But to further secure his place in the pantheon of polar explorers, he had to get there before Scott.

With no further notice than a perfunctory telegram for his rival to receive on arrival in Australia, Amundsen sailed the *Fram* to the Bay of Whales, a transient inlet in the face of the Barrier. There he set up his hut, named it Framheim, and prepared to winter over.

Since Amundsen was in it for the "win" he was concerned that Scott's motor sledges could give his "rival" explorer a significant edge in getting there first. Therefore, Amundsen was determined to start his march to the pole as soon as spring began. He set out with seven of his men, seven sledges and more than eighty dogs on September 8, 1911. Each man had his own sledge except Amundsen. Winter still wasn't as over as he had thought, and they experienced temperatures as low as -67° F (-55° C) causing frostbite and challenging sledging conditions. Unable to safely go further, they unloaded their sledges at 80° S to create a more useful depot for the future and headed back to Framheim.

Upon their return, Amundsen had a falling out with Fredrik Hjalmar Johansen, the famed Norwegian explorer who years before had accompanied Nansen in an attempt on the North Pole. Before setting out, Johansen argued with Amundsen that it was too early to start and now he was proven right, especially since on the return run for Framheim, Johansen had to stop his sledge to save the life of another expedition member who was suffering badly from the cold.

Amundsen set out again on October 20, 1911, this time with fifty-two dogs and a team of four carefully selected men, experts in skiing and dog sledding, again in a race to beat Scott to the South Pole. He purposely left Johansen behind.

Amundsen succeeded. He and his men arrived at the South Pole after a journey of nine weeks, pioneering a route up the previously unknown Axel Heiberg Glacier, to arrive with "relative ease" at the South Pole. After spending a few days there to absolutely confirm his discovery, he left a note for Scott in a tent, and headed for home. The return was "easy," if any travel across Antarctica can be characterized as such. The dogs pulled well, the weather was steady, and his team arrived safely back at Framheim on January 25, 1912 after an absence of ninety-nine days. Ironically, Scott had just reached the Pole a week earlier to discover that he had come in second, and was on that very date, January 25th, only a few days into his long and fateful return.

For Amundsen, the Pole was the goal, and he now had achieved it. All that remained was to sail with the *Fram* for Tasmania, and tell the world. Quite simply, he did what he set out to do, and in the process brought home the first proof of the discovery of the South Pole. The value of this singular feat deserves praise beyond its model of expedition planning and execution. It was a milestone in the advance of civilization. Amundsen is justly celebrated for the cool efficiency with which he adapted his plans to changing circumstances, and brought them to completion.

A few of his men were somewhat versed in the principles of meteorology and geology, but science was not the driving force behind Amundsen's plans; it was not his higher purpose. The placing of the Norwegian flag on the Pole was a worthy goal. Norway had only achieved independence from Sweden seven years before and was now entering onto the world stage. However without a strong scientific element to the expedition, it was perhaps not a lofty goal. In the end, Amundsen never could come to terms with the negative reaction expressed by the British to his secret change of plans in 1910. H.R. Mill, of the Royal Geographical Society, once described Amundsen as the most unhappy of all the polar explorers he had ever met. In a tragic footnote, Hjalmar Johansen committed suicide six months after returning to Norway in 1913.

In all this grasping for the South Pole, or for the small bits of data to add to the sum of all science, is one purpose higher than another? There is no answer. Each of us must decide for ourselves, and live with the results of our decisions.

Not every endeavor *has* to have a greater purpose, but remarkable things can come from those that do. The question, "What is your higher goal?" intends to make no judgments. It does, however, make an assumption, and expects you to have an answer. The answer will be yours alone.

What is your greater purpose?

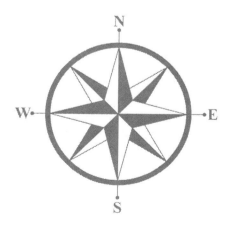

Improving Your Decision Making: Seven Lessons From The Antarctic

M any decision making lessons can be learned from the early Antarctic explorers, which relate to modern life. Although the heroic Antarctic explorers lived more than one hundred years ago, in a simpler age, their approach to adversity, risk, bad luck and dire circumstances provides much more than memorable stories. They provide real, tested in the field, timeless strategies that can be used today when facing your own challenges and decision points.

Our goal in sharing these stories is to help you improve your own decision making, and to provide new strategies for dealing with risk and adversity. One advantage of deriving these decision strategies from the Antarctic stories is that the tales are memorable; recalling a situation the explorers faced makes it easy to think about how they tackled it—a prompt from a prior century, if you will.

Here are seven of the best strategies they deployed:

1. Meet every decision point head-on. No matter how tough the circumstances were, all the men of the heroic age expeditions confronted decisions as they met them; they didn't procrastinate, and they didn't wallow in self-pity. They faced situations and quickly made decisive choices. There are many examples of this, including the spontaneous action of Frank Wild in taking charge of the remnants of an early field party to lead the men away from the icy cliff after one man fell to his death. He wasn't a leader at that point, but stepped up to take the lead. His quick thinking and decisive action saved the lives of the men he was with, as well as his own.

2. Make the best of a bad decision. A distinguishing feature of the heroic age expeditions from other polar expeditions is the number of bad decisions that were made, but from which they remarkably recovered, thanks to sheer grit and determination. For example, Shackleton's decision not to land the *Endurance* earlier was unfortunate. His choice to seek a better location along the shores of the ice-filled Weddell Sea resulted in the *Endurance* being iced in and ultimately crushed. It may have been a bad or unlucky decision, nonetheless, he and the crew made the best of the situation and all survived. Amundsen made his own unfortunate decision by starting too early in the spring in his determination to beat Scott to the South Pole. He and his team had to turn back due to severe cold, and by regrouping and starting a bit later, still managed to achieve their goal.

3. Engage others on your team. In modern life, when faced with risk, adversity or a decision point, people may think it is a sign of weak leadership to ask others for their advice. In contrast, team leadership on the early Antarctic expeditions adapted to situations as needed and sought advice where needed.

Scott depended on Edward Wilson's counsel on various decisions. Bowers, Wilson and Cherry-Garrard were a remarkable team on the "worst journey in the world." Crean, Lashly and Lt. Evans worked as a high-functioning team in their return as the last supporting Polar Party to Scott. Shackleton depended upon Frank Wild and Frank Worsley. In Antarctica, these leaders had only the few men they were with as team members. In contrast, in the modern world we can have the support and counsel of a wider "team," including family, friends, work colleagues, and others from around the world, via modern, instantaneous communication methods.

4. Inspiration can come from unexpected places. When facing challenging decision points, looking outside your immediate circumstances for inspiration can be a big help. Mawson only summoned the strength for a second try at pulling himself out of the icy crevasse when he remembered a poem. Shackleton relied on the poems by Tennyson, Browning and others to inspire himself and his men. In their cases, poetry and literature, and their legacy in letters, were more than paper and pen—these inspirations kept them alive.

5. Never, ever give up. Story after story illustrates situations where the explorers could have given up—but never did. Many felt the call of a higher purpose, and they never gave up hope, courage and determination. Nor should you, no matter how bad a situation seems.

The list of heroic age Antarctic explorers who didn't give up is almost endless.

Think of:

- Mawson down the crevasse knowing that even if he survived, he might not reach the ship in time

- Scott, Wilson and Bowers' return journey from the Pole after Edgar Evans and Captain Oates died

- Wilson, Bowers and Cherry-Garrard on "the worst journey in the world" after their tent blew away in a blizzard, facing temperatures so low they were getting frostbite in their sleeping bags (luckily they recovered the tent later that day)

- Frank Wild and the men on Elephant Island staying alive for four long months while waiting for "the Boss" to return

- Shackleton, Crean and Worsley walking across the uncharted, unexplored mountainous interior of South Georgia to the whaling station after they had to land the *James Caird* on the opposite side of the island

- Crean's epic do-or-die thirty-five-mile walk with only three biscuits and two sticks of chocolate in his pocket, and Evans surviving despite severe scurvy, thanks to Crean's rescue

- Mackintosh and the Ross Sea Party keeping their promise and laying depots despite the lack of supplies and equipment

- The Northern Party having to winter over in a snow cave with limited food, and then having to walk more than two hundred miles (320 km) back to safety when spring came.

The universal attribute was—they *never, ever* gave up, no matter how tough it got.

6. Reframe what success looks like. Sometimes fate has a way of preventing you from achieving your goal, but gives you an opportunity to reframe it. Amundsen reframed his goal of being first to the North Pole when Peary and Cook each claimed to have reached it. He adroitly reframed his goal to head south to challenge Scott. After the *Endurance* broke up, Shackleton reframed his goal of being the first to walk across continental Antarctica, to one of getting all the men from the *Endurance* home alive. During the *Nimrod* Expedition, Shackleton again proved astute at setting new milestones. He realized that he and his crew had proceeded as far south as they possibly could, and would have to turn around. They left all their supplies and tent to walk one more day south to accomplish a new goal: be the first to get within one hundred geographical miles (185 km) of the South Pole.

7. When all else fails, bad luck descends, and the end is truly in sight, how do you act nobly? Sometimes it really is the end. Scott, Wilson, and Bowers gave it their best shot. They achieved the South Pole, but arrived a month and three days after Amundsen. Amundsen had led an exemplary expedition—well planned and well executed. In comparison, some might have argued Scott didn't stand a chance of getting there first, but Scott, Wilson and Bowers left us another legacy. They acted nobly right up to the end. They dutifully carried Amundsen's letter addressed to the King of Norway with them. Though suffering from frostbite and starvation, they never abandoned the Antarctic rocks they had collected that were vital to the scientific exploration that their expedition prided itself on.

And, at the very end, they wrote poignant, memorable and noble letters to their sponsors and loved ones, and left us with these immortal words:

> "Had we lived, I should have had a tale to tell of the hardihood, endurance, and courage of my companions which would have stirred the heart of every Englishman."—*Robert Scott, 1912.*

And those rocks—the heavy manifestation of the credo of science above all, collected and carried along with them to the very end—contained the first recorded Antarctic fossil of a distinctive fern plant. They helped prove that the Southern Continents were once linked, yielding the vital scientific evidence needed to establish the theories of continental drift and plate tectonics. The value of their expedition, and the other heroic age expeditions, lives on to this day.

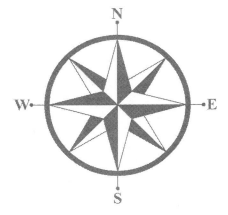

Tables

Ships and Huts

Expedition Name/ Date/Leader	Ship	Hut	Hut Location	What is visible today
Discovery Expedition (1901-1904) Scott	*Discovery* (Relief/rescue ships: *Morning* and *Terra Nova*)	Discovery Hut	Hut Point, Cape Evans	Discovery Hut still standing. The *Discovery* is at Discovery Point which is a museum in Dundee, Scotland.
Nimrod Expedition (1907-1909) Shackleton	*Nimrod*	Shackleton's Hut	Cape Royds	Shackleton's Hut still standing. The *Nimrod* sank off coast of Norfolk, England in 1919.
Terra Nova Expedition (1910-1913) Scott	*Terra Nova*	Terra Nova Hut (also known as Scott's Hut)	Cape Evans *Also Northern Party over-wintered at Cape Adare, then went to Evans Cove. Winter Journey went to Cape Crozier.*	Terra Nova Hut still standing. The *Terra Nova* sank off the Greenland coast in 1943.
Norwegian Antarctic Expedition (1910-1912) Amundsen	*Fram*	Framheim	Bay of Whales, (Ross Ice Shelf)	Framheim no longer exists. The *Fram* is in the Fram Museum in Oslo, Norway.
Australian Antarctic Expedition (1911-1914) Mawson	*Aurora*	Mawson's Huts	Cape Denison, Commonwealth Bay *Also Western Base Party was based at Queen Mary Land.*	Mawson's Huts are still standing. The *Aurora* sank in 1917 en route from Australia to Chile.
Endurance Expedition *Official Name:* Imperial Trans-Antarctic Expedition (1914-1917) Shackleton	*Endurance* (Weddell Sea side) *Aurora* (Ross Sea Party)	The *Endurance* never landed so no hut was built. Ross Sea Party used the Terra Nova Hut at Cape Evans as well as Discovery Hut.		The *Endurance* was crushed in the ice. The *James Caird* survived and is on display at Dulwich College, England. The *Aurora* sank in 1917 en route from Australia to Chile.

Key people, the expeditions they participated in, and summary information on their decision making

This is not a comprehensive list of personnel. It simply provides an aid for keeping track of key expedition members mentioned in our chapters.

Person	Expeditions	Key Decisions & Other Useful Information
Roald Amundsen	Norwegian Antarctic Expedition	Discovered the Northwest Passage. Leader of the Norwegian Antarctic Expedition. First to the South Pole.
Olaf Bjaaland	Norwegian Antarctic Expedition	Expert skier on Norwegian Antarctic Expedition. Accompanied Amundsen to the South Pole.
Henry 'Birdie' Bowers	*Terra Nova* Expedition	Went with Wilson and Cherry-Garrard on the Winter Journey in search of emperor penguin eggs. Died with Scott and Wilson in their tent, 11 miles from One Ton depot, on the way back from the South Pole.
Victor Campbell	*Terra Nova* Expedition	Leader of the Northern Party who had to over-winter in an ice cave.
Apsley Cherry-Garrard	*Terra Nova* Expedition	Went with Wilson and Bowers on the Winter Journey in search of emperor penguin eggs. Part of the group that decided to search for Scott's remains rather than try to rescue the Northern Party. **Author of *The Worst Journey in the World*.**
Tom Crean	*Discovery* Expedition *Terra Nova* Expedition *Endurance* Expedition	With Lt. Evans and William Lashly, the last returning support party to Scott's journey to the South Pole. On the *Endurance* Expedition was one of the six men in the *James Caird* voyage from Elephant Island to South Georgia. He trekked across the uncharted South Georgia mountains with Shackleton and Worsley.
Edgar Evans	*Discovery* Expedition *Terra Nova* Expedition	Petty Officer on the *Discovery*; with Scott and Lashly explored the Antarctic Plateau and discovered the Dry Valleys in 1903. Member of Scott's five-man Polar Party. Died after a fall during the return journey from the South Pole.
Lt. Edward (Teddy) Evans	*Discovery* Expedition *Terra Nova* Expedition	Second Officer on the *Morning* relief ship for the *Discovery* Expedition. Second in command on the *Terra Nova* Expedition. Leader of the last supporting party for Scott's attempt on the South Pole on the *Terra Nova* Expedition. Almost died of scurvy on return journey with Crean and Lashly.
Fredrik Hjalmar Johansen	Norwegian Antarctic Expedition	Legendary Norwegian polar explorer who had accompanied Nansen on a North Pole expedition. Challenged Amundsen about setting out too early, resulting in Amundsen refusing to take him in the Polar Party when he set out a second time.
Ernest Joyce	*Discovery* Expedition *Nimrod* Expedition *Endurance* Expedition (Ross Sea Party)	Key member of the Ross Sea Party. Assumed leadership at key moments.

Key people, the expeditions they participated in, and summary information on their decision making (continued)

Person	Expeditions	Key Decisions & Other Useful Information
William Lashly	*Discovery* Expedition *Terra Nova* Expedition	Member of the last returning support party for Scott's journey to the South Pole. Lashly stayed behind with Lt. Evans, when Crean set off on his 35-mile trek to seek rescue for them.
Aeneas Mackintosh	*Nimrod* Expedition *Endurance* Expedition	While unloading the *Nimrod*, a hook swung and hit him in the eye, causing him to lose the eye. He therefore had to give up his place in the *Nimrod* Expedition shore party. Leader of the *Endurance* Expedition Ross Sea Party. Died with Victor Hayward when they crossed thin ice, after having survived near death by scurvy on the Ross Sea Party.
Douglas Mawson	*Nimrod* Expedition Australian Antarctic Expedition	Geologist and professor. First to discover the South Magnetic Pole (with Edgeworth David and Alistair Mackay). Leader of the Australian Antarctic Expedition. Survived on his own with limited supplies after the deaths of Xavier Mertz and Belgrave Ninnis.
Lawrence 'Titus' Oates	*Terra Nova* Expedition	One of Scott's five-man team which went to the South Pole. Famously walked out of the tent to his death knowing his debilitating frostbite would slow Bowers, Scott and Wilson and risk their survival.
Robert Scott	*Discovery* Expedition *Terra Nova* Expedition	Led the most scientific expeditions in Antarctica during the heroic age. Leader of the *Discovery* Expedition. With Wilson and Shackleton acheived furthest south on the *Discovery* Expedition. Also discovered and explored parts of the Antarctic Plateau. As leader of the *Terra Nova* Expedition, he reached the South Pole and perished on his return from it. The Scott Polar Research Institute is named in his honor.
Ernest Shackleton	*Discovery* Expedition *Terra Nova* Expedition *Endurance* Expedition	Leader of the *Nimrod* Expedition. Discovered a route through the Beardmore Glacier to reach the Polar Plateau. Achieved the furthest south on the *Nimrod* Expedition. Leader of the *Endurance* Expedition. Ensured all the men from the *Endurance* survived after the ship was crushed in the ice, by achieving the daring 800-mile open boat journey to South Georgia in the *James Caird*. Shackleton died on the *Quest* Expedition in January 1922 and is buried in Grytviken, South Georgia.

Key people, the expeditions they participated in, and summary information on their decision making (continued)

Person	Expeditions	Key Decisions & Other Useful Information
Frank Wild	*Discovery* Expedition *Nimrod* Expedition Australian Antarctic Expedition *Endurance* Expedition	Leader of the Western Base Party on the Australian Antarctic Expedition. Leader of twent-two men stranded on Elephant Island during the *Endurance* Expedition. Spent six winters in the Antarctic. Awarded five Polar medals (one for the *Quest* Expedition in 1922) (Ernest Wild, his brother, was part of the Ross Sea Party.)
Edward Wilson	*Discovery* Expedition *Terra Nova* Expedition	Medical doctor, scientist, artist. Assistant Doctor and Vertebrate Zoologist on the *Discovery* Expedition. Chief of Scientific Staff on the *Terra Nova* Expedition. Leader of the Winter Journey (*The Worst Journey in the World*) in search of emperor penguin eggs. Died with Scott and Bowers on their way back from the South Pole.
Frank Worsley	*Endurance* Expedition	Captain of the *Endurance* and part of the six-man crew on the *James Caird*. He successfully navigated the *James Caird* from Elephant Island to South Georgia. With Crean and Shackleton walked across the uncharted Southn Georgia mountains to safety.

Examples of some of the many highly effective teams

Expedition Name/ Date/Leader	Team	Number of People	Accomplishments
Discovery Expedition (1901-1904) Scott	Furthest south: Scott (leader), Shackleton, Wilson	3	First team to venture far into the Antarctic interior. Set furthest south record: 82°17'S.
Nimrod Expedition (1907-1909) Shackleton	Furthest south: Shackleton (leader), Wild, Marshall, Adams	4	This team surpassed the *Discovery* Expedition's furthest south. They reached to within 97 nautical miles of the South Pole.
Nimrod Expedition (1907-1909) Shackleton	Magnetic South Pole: Mawson (leader), David, Mackay	3	First team to reach the Magnetic South Pole.
Norwegian Antarctic Expedition (1910-1912) Amundsen	Polar Party: Amundsen (leader), Bjaaland, Hanssen, Hassel, Wisting	5	First team to reach the South Pole.
Terra Nova Expedition (1910-1913) Scott	Winter Journey: Wilson (leader), Bowers, Cherry-Garrard	3	Collected emperor penguin eggs in the middle of the Antarctic winter.
Terra Nova Expedition (1910-1913) Scott	Polar Party: Scott (leader), Wilson, Bowers, Oates, Evans	5	Second team to reach the South Pole, thirty-four days after Amundsen's team. Collected geologically valuable fossil specimens during their return.
Terra Nova Expedition (1910-1913) Scott	Northern Party: Campbell (leader), Priestley, Levick, Abbott, Browning, Dickason	6	Survived over-wintering in an ice cave.
Terra Nova Expedition (1910-1913) Scott	Last Supporting Party: Lt. Evans (leader), Crean, Lashly	3	Last supporting party for Scott's polar team.
Terra Nova Expedition (1910-1913) Scott	Search Party: Atkinson (leader)	12	Made the decision to seek Scott's tent rather than attempt to rescue the Northern Party.
Australian Antarctic Expedition (1911-1914) Mawson	Eastern Coastal Party: Mawson (leader), Ninnis, Mertz	3	Eastern coastal survey. Strong team until Ninnis, then Mertz perished.

Examples of some of the many highly effective teams (continued)

Expedition Name/ Date/Leader	Team	Number of People	Situation
Endurance Expedition (1914-1917) Shackleton	*Endurance* crew: Shackleton (leader)	28	Entire crew survived months on ice floes after the *Endurance* sank.
Endurance Expedition (1914-1917) Shackleton	*Dudley Docker* Lifeboat crew: Worsley (leader)	9	Successfully sailed and rowed from the Patience Camp ice floe to Elephant Island.
Endurance Expedition (1914-1917) Shackleton	*Stancomb Wills* Lifeboat crew: Crean (leader)	8	Successfully sailed and rowed from the Patience Camp ice floe to Elephant Island.
Endurance Expedition (1914-1917) Shackleton	*James Caird* Lifeboat crew: Shackleton (leader)	11	Successfully sailed and rowed from the Patience Camp ice floe to Elephant Island.
Endurance Expedition (1914-1917) Shackleton	*James Caird* voyage across Southern Ocean: Shackleton (leader), Worsley (Captain), Crean, McCarthy, McNish, Vincent	6	Successfully sailed 800 miles from Elephant Island to South Georgia across some of the roughest seas in the world.
Endurance Expedition (1914-1917) Shackleton	Trek across South Georgia: Shackleton (leader), Crean, Worsley	3	Successfully achieved the first trek across the interior mountains of South Georgia.
Endurance Expedition (1914-1917) Shackleton	Men left on Elephant Island: Frank Wild (leader)	22	Survived four-and-a-half months on rocky uninhabited island.
Endurance Expedition (1914-1917) Shackleton	Ross Sea Party: Aeneas Mackintosh (leader) and at times Ernest Joyce served as leader	10	Laid depots to Beardmore Glacier despite limited supplies and enormous hardship.

Appendix I

Authors' note on the expeditions of the heroic era of Antarctic exploration

The term "heroic era" was coined by the Reverend J. Gordon Hayes for his 1932 book, *The Conquest of the South Pole*. His concept has taken hold, and the heroic era is today most often construed as beginning with Scott's *Discovery* Expedition in 1901, ending with the return of Shackleton's *Endurance* Expedition (officially named as the Imperial Trans-Antarctic Expedition) in 1917. Mechanized transport and radio communication had yet to be perfected. Ponies, dogs, and men moved the supplies overland, leaving notes and detailed instructions along the way. They put their trust in experience, luck, and dogged determination to help them survive when these broke down.

There were also several expeditions in the field a few years prior to 1901, including the *Belgica's* long winter beset in the pack ice of the Ross Sea in 1898, and Carsten Borchgrevink's *Southern Cross* Expedition, the first to winter on the Antarctic mainland in 1900. Although these endeavors demonstrated the possibility of extended stays amid the ice and darkness, neither made significant forays into the continent's interior. They provided the first Antarctic baselines of weather, ice, and magnetic observation that have become the foundation of today's physical sciences in that region.

There were other expeditions that were active during those years. Germany's *Gauss* Expedition, under Captain Erich von Drygalski, operated in the Antarctic concurrently with Scott's *Discovery* and Sweden's Antarctic Expeditions to study terrestrial magnetism and other physical phenomena in 1901-1903. Germany sent another ship in 1911-1912, the *Deutschland* under Wilhelm Filchner. Both explored previously undiscovered parts of the Antarctic coast. Japan sent the *Kainan Maru* in 1910-1912. It landed a shore party at the Bay of Whales alongside Amundsen's Framheim, and ventured over the Great Ice Barrier into the foothills of King Edward VII Land.

The authors fully recognize the contributions of these expeditions, and the men who risked their lives to fulfil them, but this book does not pretend to be a history of Antarctic exploration. It seeks instead to look at the work of a few, those to whom the word "heroic" most applies, whose men endured more than ordinary mortals could be expected to, and for the most part, survived. Many of them returned to the Antarctic to live the life once again, face the risks, and overcome adversity by sheer unstoppable endurance.

Their stories are very compelling. They serve as object lessons to those of us today who face our own adversities, and are willing to give our all to overcome them.

Appendix II

Additional information about Antarctic places and phrases used in this book

Aurora: Ship used first on Mawson's Australian Antarctic Expedition, 1911-1914, and later by Shackleton's *Endurance* Expedition (also known as the Imperial Trans-Antarctic Expedition), 1914-1917, to transport the Ross Sea Party.

Balloon Bight: An inlet in the Great Ice Barrier first discovered by Scott's *Discovery* Expedition in 1902, and named for the first aerial balloon ascent in Antarctica. It subsequently changed dramatically in form, and was renamed by Shackleton to the Bay of Whales.

Barrier or *Great Ice Barrier* (today called the *Ross Ice Shelf*): An enormous sheet of floating ice, as large as France, filling the area between Ross Island and the Antarctic continent to the south. Its seaward face runs east from Cape Crozier to King Edward VII Land in a bluff hundreds of feet high in places. It prevented ships from reaching land but provided a long level route to the Beardmore Glacier and Axel Heiberg Glacier, both of which lead to the Polar Plateau.

Bay of Whales: Shackleton declined to land there in 1907, fearing a catastrophic calving of the Barrier, while Amundsen felt confident in its stability and made Framheim there in 1911.

Beardmore Glacier: A massive river of ice twenty miles (32 km) wide and 120 miles (193 km) long, leading from the Barrier to the South Polar Plateau. Discovered by Shackleton in 1908, this glacier was the highway to the interior later used by Scott's *Terra Nova* Expedition.

Biscuit: An Antarctic biscuit is a simple type of thick cracker made from wholemeal flour, water, and sometimes salt. This part of the overall sledging ration was inexpensive and long-lasting. They had some nutritional value (B vitamins, etc.) and importantly provided roughage to the sledging diet. For the *Terra Nova* Expedition, Dr. Edward Wilson had the biscuits made from his own recipe to improve their nutritional value, but his recipe was not written in his diaries and has now been lost.

Blubber: A thick layer of fat found under the skin of all whales, seals and penguins. Once it has been rendered, it can serve as fuel for cooking and lighting, and can be consumed as food for humans.

Cairn: A temporary monument of snow blocks piled one on top of the other and used to mark trails the explorers took. This made it easier for the explorers to find their way back, or for others to follow in their path.

***Cape Adare*:** The northernmost landing site on the coast of Victoria Land, and site of the wintering parties of Borchgrevink's *Southern Cross* Expedition 1898-1900, and Scott's Northern Party from the *Terra Nova* Expedition (1911). The Northern Party made use of Borchgrevink's huts, which were still standing.

***Cape Crozier*:** The easternmost point of Ross Island, the site of the largest emperor penguin breeding colony, and the western terminus of the Great Ice Barrier.

***Cape Denison*:** The name given to the land at Commonwealth Bay where Mawson established his home base on the Australian Antarctic Expedition, 1911-1914. It is one of the windiest places in the world with wind speeds of up to two hundred miles/hour (320km/h).

***Cape Evans*:** Site of Scott's home base during the *Terra Nova* Expedition, 1910-1913. It is on the west side of Ross Island, facing McMurdo Sound. It was later used as home base by the Shackleton's Ross Sea Party 1914-1916.

Crevasse: A deep, usually vertical, crack or split in a glacier, formed as the brittle ice flows over an uneven surface beneath the ice. Crevasses, even wide ones, can become covered over by blown snow. These "lids" are not easily seen and can give out without warning beneath an explorer. Over time these lids may fall away, leaving narrow bridges across the deep crevasses.

Discovery: Ship used on Scott's first expedition, the *Discovery* Expedition, 1901-1904.

Discovery Hut: Hut built at Hut Point on Cape Evans for Scott's *Discovery* Expedition, 1901-1904 and used as shelter by most of the expeditions that followed.

Elephant Island: One of the easternmost of the South Shetland Islands, where twenty-two of Shackleton's *Endurance* party were marooned in 1916.

Evans Cove: Inlet on the shore of Victoria Land, where Scott's Northern Party had been dropped off by the *Terra Nova* to explore the local area for six weeks. The ship was unable to penetrate the ice to pick them up and the six men had to spend the winter in an ice cave on Inexpressible Island.

Finnesko: Boots made entirely from reindeer skin, with the fur on the outside.

Floe: A discrete piece of flat, floating sea ice separated from its neighbors by lanes of open water. Depending on the age and local pack conditions, a floe's size may range from a couple dozen yards to miles in extent. Unlike an icefield, when navigating a ship, an ice floe's extent can be distinguished from the ship's masthead.

Fram: Polar exploration ship commissioned by Fridtjof Nansen and designed and built by famed Norwegian naval shipbuilder Colin

Archer in 1892. It was later used by Amundsen for his Norwegian Antarctic Expedition, 1910-1912.

Framheim: Amundsen's home base in 1910-1912, near the Bay of Whales.

Glacier: A river of ice, generally flowing down a valley, with rock walls at either side. Glaciers can be small valley glaciers, ice streams, or immense flows like the Beardmore at one hundred and twenty miles (193 km) long from its head at the South Polar Plateau (ten thousand feet above sea level) to the Barrier, and up to twenty miles (32 km) in width. The surface of a glacier is split into multitudes of deep crevasses.

Great Ice Barrier: (see Barrier)

Harness: A broad canvas upper body belt used in man-hauling sledges. As seen in many expedition photographs such as the one on the cover of this book, teams of men worked together to pull one sledge. On occasion, when someone fell into a crevasse, his harness and tether to the sledge were what saved him.

Hoosh: A single-pot stew, heated over a Primus stove. Made from pemmican (dried and powdered meat) and grains; it may also include blubber, and any other edibles that may be at hand.

Hummock: A mass of sea ice rising to a considerable height, often up to forty feet above the general level of a floe. Hummocks are created by the pressure of floes driven by wind and current to grind against each other.

Hut Point: Landfall near the westernmost point of Ross Island, where the *Discovery* spent the winters of 1902 and 1903, and site of the Discovery Hut, which served subsequent Antarctic explorers as well.

Ice Cap: A dome-shaped cover of perennial ice and snow, covering the summit area of a mountain mass so that no peaks emerge through it. The South Polar Plateau where the South Pole is located is an ice cap of continental dimension, at an average elevation of ten thousand feet above sea level. This ice cap is two miles (3.2 km) thick.

Lead: Another name for lane or channel through the floes of floating sea ice. A ship is said to "take the right lead" when she follows a channel conducting her into a more navigable water.

Magnetic South Pole: (As distinct from the South Pole, which is also called the South Geographic Pole). The Magnetic South Pole is the one place in the entire Southern Hemisphere, where a magnetic dip needle would point down into a straight vertical line. It was discovered by Mawson, Edgeworth David and Alistair Mackay as a result of a challenging trek taken on the *Nimrod* Expedition in 1909.

Man-hauling: Moving heavily laden sledges over the ice by men in harness. Man-hauling at high altitude in polar conditions is one of the most physically demanding efforts known. The caloric intake required to perform the work and maintain body heat is about 6,500 calories per day, requiring an enormous intake of food. Scott recognized the need for high-energy foods but seriously underestimated the necessary caloric intake. His Summit Ration provided about 4,500 calories per day. The men were eating their full ration, and slowly starving themselves.

McMurdo Sound: Body of water between Ross Island and the southern coast of Victoria Land, discovered by James Clark Ross in 1841. Hut Point lies at its southern extremity, and Cape Evans looks over it from the east.

Morning: Relief ship used on Scott's *Discovery* Expedition, 1901-1904.

Motor Sledge: Not really a sledge, but a motor tractor on caterpillar treads intended to pull loaded sledges. Scott's experimental use of them was not a great success, but it did establish the value of these tracked vehicles for later Antarctic exploration. His motor sledges were the forerunner to the treaded tanks designed for WW1 and the basis for modern polar vehicles.

Mount Erebus: The world's southernmost active volcano; this smoking mountain on Ross Island overlooks the historic sites of Scott's and Shackleton's expeditions.

Nansen Cooker: A mountain so deeply buried in ice that only its upper part remains in view as exposed rock. As one ascends the Polar Plateau, these last vestiges of the coastal mountain ranges eventually disappear from view.

Nimrod: Ship used by Shackleton's British Antarctic Expedition, 1907-1909 (also known as the *Nimrod* Expedition)

Nunatak: An exposed ridge, rock formation or small mountain rising above a glacier area, or an ice and snow encrusted area. It often has a jagged surface.

Pack Ice: Also known as sea ice. Pack ice is frozen sea that formed somewhere else and has floated to its present position due to wind, tides and currents. It is broken into floes of variable size and thickness—some pieces can be the size of a coffee table and about one foot thick; other pieces can be many acres in extent and over thirty feet thick. **Open pack**—when the pieces of ice don't touch each other; **Closed pack**—when the pieces of ice touch.

Pemmican: Meat cured, pulverized, and mixed with fat, containing much nutriment in a small compact form. It is a dense, high protein food that could be stored and transported easily.

Polar Plateau: A plain of solid ice, up to two miles (3.2 km) high, that surrounds the South Pole for hundreds of miles.

Primus Stove: A pressurized-burner kerosene (paraffin) stove that was highly reliable and durable in adverse conditions. It was the stove of choice for Shackleton's and Scott's expeditions.

Ross Ice Shelf: (see Barrier)

Ross Sea: A southern portion of the Antarctic Ocean, extending south to McMurdo Sound. Discovered in 1841 by James Clark Ross, and named in his honor.

Sea Ice: A general term for any ice that forms from frozen seawater. Sea ice covers large parts of polar waters in the winter, melting back each summer. Ice which covers an ocean or sea includes mostly continuous pack ice, broken only by narrow open water *"leads"* and discrete ice floes.

Siberian Pony: Used by Shackleton in his *Nimrod* Expedition, 1907-1909, for the transport of loaded sledges over the ice. His relative success with them prompted Scott to use Siberian ponies in his *Terra Nova* Expedition, 1910-1913.

Sledge: Made from wooden frames and runners bound with rawhide lashings to allow flexibility in transit over uneven ice, they were the principal means of transport in the Antarctic, whether pulled by men, dogs, ponies, or motors.

Sledge Dog: Dog teams were used by all the expeditions for the transport of loaded sledges, most successfully by Amundsen in his attainment of the South Pole in 1911.

South Georgia: Island at the convergence of the South Atlantic and

Antarctic Oceans, site of whaling stations, site of departure of Shackleton's *Endurance* in 1914, and landing site of the *James Caird* after an eight-hundred-mile open boat journey.

South Pole (Also known as the *South Geographic Pole*, as distinct from the *Magnetic South Pole*): Southernmost point on earth, axis of the planet's rotation, located on the Polar Plateau hundreds of miles from any point of the Antarctic coastline.

***Stromness, South Georgia*:** Whaling station on the island of South Georgia.

***Terra Nova*:** Ship used by Scott's second expedition, the *Terra Nova* Expedition, 1910-1913. She was also used as one of the relief ships for the *Discovery* Expedition, 1901-1904.

***Weddell Sea*:** A southern portion of the Antarctic Ocean, extending south to Vahsel Bay, where Shackleton intended to start his trans-Antarctic crossing.

Appendix III

Recommended reading

Have we whetted your appetite to learn more about the heroic age expeditions? Below is a list of books and films that we have enjoyed and recommend if you are interested in learning more about this fascinating era. Stars (★) have been added to highlight our top recommendations.

Published expedition diaries or accounts by the leaders of the expeditions

Roald Amundsen

* *The South Pole: An Account of the Norwegian Antarctic Expedition in the "Fram": 1910-1912*, Roald Amundsen (Indy Publishing, 2002) originally published in 1912

Douglas Mawson

* *The Home of the Blizzard: A Heroic Tale of Antarctic Exploration and Survival*, Sir Douglas Mawson, (Skyhorse 2013) originally published in 1915

Robert Scott

* *The Voyage of the "Discovery,"* Captain Robert Scott (Wordsworth, 2009) originally published in 1905

* *Scott's Last Expedition*, Captain Robert Scott (arranged by Leonard Huxley) originally published in 1914—Volume 1 is the journals of Captain Scott; Volume 2 contains the reports of the sledge journeys and the scientific work by Dr. Edward Wilson and the surviving members of the expedition

Ernest Shackleton

* *The Heart of the Antarctic*, Ernest Shackleton (Wordsworth, 2007) originally published in 1909

* *South: The Endurance Expedition*, Ernest Shackleton (Penguin, 2013) originally published in 1919

Expedition photographs and pictures

- ★ *Discovery Illustrated: Pictures from Captain Scott's First Antarctic Expedition*, Judy Skelton, David Wilson (Reardon Publishing, 2001)

- *Edward Wilson's Antarctic Notebooks*, David Wilson, Christopher Wilson (Reardon Publishing, 2011)

- *Nimrod Illustrated: Pictures from Lieutenant Shackleton's British Antarctic Expedition*, David Wilson (Reardon Publishing, 2009)

- *Scott's Last Voyage: Through the Antarctic Camera of Herbert Ponting*, Ann Savours (editor), (Sidgwick & Jackson, 1974)

- *South with Endurance: Shackleton's Antarctic Expedition 1914-1917—the Photographs of Frank Hurley*, Frank Hurley and Tamiko Rex, (Bloomsbury Publishing, 2001)

- *The Amundsen Photographs*, Captain Roald Amundsen, Roland Huntsford (editor), (Hodder & Stoughton, 1987)

- *The Enduring Eye: The Antarctic Legacy of Sir Ernest Shackleton and Frank Hurley*, Meredith Hooper (curator) (Syon Publishing, 2015)

- *The Heart of the Great Alone: Scott, Shackleton and Antarctic Photography*, David Hempleman-Adams and Sophie Gordon (The Royal Collection, 2011)

- ★ *The Lost Photographs of Captain Scott*, Dr. David Wilson, (Little Brown, 2011)

- *With Scott to the Pole: Terra Nova Expedition 1910-1913 – The Photographs of Herbert Ponting*, Herbert Ponting, Ranulph Fiennes (foreword), (Ted Smart, 2004)

Detailed accounts of the expeditions

- *Mawson's Will: The Greatest Polar Survival Story Ever Written*, Lennard Bickel (Steerforth Press, 2000)

- *Racing with Death: Douglas Mawson—Antarctic Explorer*, Beau Riffenburgh (Bloomsbury Publishing, 2009)

- *Shackleton's Boat: The Story of the James Caird*, Harding Dunnett (Collins Press, 2015)

- *Shackleton's Boat Journey*, Frank Worsley (Collins Press, 2010) originally published in 1924

- *Shackleton's Epic: Recreating the World's Greatest Journey of Survival*, Tim Jarvis, (William Collins, 2013)

- *Shackleton's Forgotten Men: The Untold Tale of an Antarctic Tragedy*, Lennard Bickel (Pimlico, 2001)

- *The Coldest March: Scott's Fatal Antarctic Expedition*, Susan Solomon (Yale University Press, 2002)

- *The Endurance—Shackleton's Legendary Antarctic Expedition*, Caroline Alexander (Bloomsbury Publishing, 1999)

★ *The Lost Men: The Harrowing Story of Shackleton's Ross Sea Party*, Kelly Tyler-Lewis (Bloomsbury, 2007)

- *The Longest Winter: Scott's Other Heroes*, Meredith Hooper (John Murray, 2011)

★ *The Worst Journey in the World*, Apsley Cherry-Garrard (Vintage Classics, 2010) originally published in 1922

Biographies of explorers

- *An Unsung Hero: Tom Crean—Antarctic Survivor*, Michael Smith (Collins Press, 2009)

- *Antarctic Voyager: Tom Crean with Scott's Discovery Expedition 1901-1904*, David Hirzel, (Terra Nova Press, 2015)

- *Birdie Bowers: Captain Scott's Marvel*, Anne Strathie, (The History Press, 2013)

- *Captain Scott*, Sir Ranulph Fiennes (Hodder Paperbacks, 2004)

- *Captain Scott's Invaluable Assistant: Edgar Evans*, Isobel Williams, (The History Press, 2012)

- *Cheltenham in Antarctica: The Life of Edward Wilson*, David Wilson and David Elder, (Reardon Publishing, 2000)

- *Cherry: A Life of Apsley Cherry-Garrard*, Sara Wheeler, (Vintage, 2002)

- *Hold Fast: Tom Crean with Shackleton in the Antarctic 1914-1916*, David Hirzel (Terra Nova Press, 2013)

- *I Am Just Going Outside: The Tragedy of Captain Oates*, Michael Smith, (Spellmount, 2002)

- *Sailor on Ice: Tom Crean with Scott in the Antarctic 1910-1913*, David Hirzel, (Terra Nova Press, 2011)

- *Scott of the Antarctic: The Definitive Biography*, David Crane, (Harper, 2012)

- *Shackleton*, Margery and James Fisher (Barrie, 1957)

- *Shackleton: An Irishman in Antarctica*, Jonathan Shackleton and John MacKenna, (Lilliput Press, 2003)

★ *Shackleton: By Endurance We Conquer*, Michael Smith, (Collins Press, 2014)

- *The Quest for Frank Wild*, Angie Butler, (Jackleberry Press, 2011)

- *With Scott in the Antarctic: Edward Wilson: Explorer, Naturalist, Artist*, Isobel Williams, (The History Press, 2009)

Other relevant books about historic Antarctic exploration

* *Conquest of the South Pole: Antarctic Exploration 1906-1931*, J. Gordon Hayes (Thornton Butterworth, 1932)

* *Scott and Charcot at the col du Lautaret—1908 Trials of the first motor driven sledges designed for transport in the Antarctic*, Serge Aubert, Judy Skelton, Yves Frenot, and Alain Bignon (Lautaret, 2014)

Books about Antarctica, not specific to expeditions

* *Antarctica: An Intimate Portrait of the World's Most Mysterious Continent*, Gabrielle Walker, (Bloomsbury, 2013)

* *The Storied Ice: Exploration, Discovery, and Adventure in Antarctica's Peninsula Region*, Joan Boothe (Regent Press, 2011)

* *Terra Incognita: Travels in Antarctica*, Sara Wheeler, (Vintage, 1997)

Other books relating the Antarctic experience to business management

* *Shackleton's Way: Leadership Lessons from the Great Antarctic Explorer*, Margot Morrell and Stephanie Capparell (Nicholas Brealey, 2003)

* *Leading at the Edge: Leadership Lessons from the Extraordinary Saga of Shackleton's Antarctic Expedition*, Dennis Perkins (Amacom, 2000)

Films and DVDs

★ *Scott Of The Antarctic*, Director: Charles Frend, Main actor: John Mills, (Studio: Ealing Studios) originally released in 1948, now available on DVD

★ *Shackleton*, Director: Charles Sturridge,
Main actor: Kenneth Branagh, (Studio: Channel 4)
DVD released in 2008

★ *Shackleton—Death Or Glory*: Recreation of Shackleton's
boat journey. Expedition leader: Tim Jarvis,
(Studio: Discovery Channel) DVD released in 2014

• *South [1919]*, Director: Frank Hurley, featuring real footage
shot by Hurley on the Endurance Expedition

• *The Endurance: Shackleton's Legendary Antarctic Expedition*,
Actor: Liam Neeson, (Studio: Sony Pictures)
DVD released in 2003

• *The Great White Silence / 90 Degrees South*, Director: Herbert
Ponting with Robert Scott, (Studio: BFI Video)
Originally released in 1933, featuring real footage shot by
Ponting on the Terra Nova Expedition.

Acknowledgements

The authors would like to acknowledge the wide array of experts in the fields of Antarctic exploration and book production, who have lent their cumulative knowledge and friendship to the support of this endeavor.

At the top of the list is the world-renowned Antarctic historian Dr. David Wilson (grand-nephew of Dr. Edward Wilson). David Wilson's lectures and books on Antarctica have served as an inspiration for us and reinforced our desire to bring the stories to a wider audience. We are sincerely and deeply honored that he has written the foreword to our book.

Also, high on this list is Robert Stephenson, whose notable website *www.antarctic-circle.org* has provided an online forum for a worldwide net of Antarctic enthusiasts. Robert created and hosted the "SouthPole-sium" conference in May 2015 in Craobh Haven, Scotland, at the suggestion of Falcon Scott (grandson of Robert Scott), which brought many of us from around the world. It was here that the authors met for the first time, and brainstormed the idea for this book.

As the authors labored over the text of the book during the following year, Shari Powell helped to refine our ideas into a coherent and meaningful book, and Anne Sharples gave it a striking cover and interior design. Long conversations with Alice Cochran on the nature of leadership and decision making have left their inevitable mark. Their unflagging support has molded the authors' collection of chapters and ideas into its final shape, and it is to them that we owe great thanks and appreciation.

This field of study is overflowing with scholars, explorers, and enthusiasts, many of whom have become friends over the years. Their thoughts and ideas have contributed to our own, and their invisible presence has helped to make this book. We must mention first the annual Shackleton Autumn School conference in Athy, Ireland hosted at the Athy Heritage Center and organized by Francis Taaffe, Seamus Taaffe, Kevin Kenny, Joe O'Farrell and Margaret Walsh. This is a wonderful and informative event. We deeply appreciate their friendship and warmth, as well as the many evenings with them in O'Brien's pub discussing all things related to Antarctica and polar exploration. The next round of drinks is on us!

Over the years, we have had the pleasure of meeting and learning from world-renowned authors, historians and lecturers specializing in the field, including Bob Burton, Angie Butler, Bob Headland, Stephen Scott-Fawcett, Alexandra Shackleton (grand-daughter of Sir Ernest Shackleton), Jonathan Shackleton (cousin of Sir Ernest Shackleton), Judy Skelton (grand-daughter of Reginald Skelton from the *Discovery* Expedition), Michael Smith, Anne Strathie, Michael Tarver and David Wilson. Our recommended reading list has space for only a few of these many excellent books. Joan N. Boothe gave us access to her extensive private Antarctic library for research, and her photography graces some of the pages of this book.

We are also grateful to the many people we have met, learned from, and become friends with over our many years' interest in polar exploration. These include Cathy Cooper, Wendy Driver, Valerie and Donald Kerr (grandson of Alexander Kerr who was the second engineer on the *Endurance* Expedition), Jim and Geraldine McAdam, Cathy Corbishley Michel, Geoff Michel, Susan Morrison, Katie Murray and Sam Richmond.

Among the rare book dealers who not only specialize in the polar books, but are themselves authors and producers of conferences and book fairs, and have a wealth of knowledge, we take special note of our friends John and Suzanne Bonham of J&SL Bonham Books in London, Paul Davies of Kingsbridge Books, Stuart Leggett of Meridian Rare Books, and Chet Ross of Chet Ross Rare Books. We have also had the honor to meet and attend lectures by modern day explorers Tim Jarvis and Sebastian Coulthard, who were part of the six-man team that recreated Shackleton's boat journey and trek across South Georgia in 2013.

The Scott Polar Research Institute in Cambridge, England, is a treasure trove of information and the leading repository of manuscripts and artifacts of Antarctic exploration. The semi-annual meetings of the James Caird Society at Dulwich College (where Shackleton went to school) provided a wonderful way to learn from experts while mingling with modern day adventurers. The publications and meetings of these institutions continue to promote the study of the heroic age.

Special thanks to Professor Howard Kunreuther who taught Decision Sciences at the Wharton School, and was so kind as to list Brad Borkan as a co-author on several of his books about the study of people's decision making related to low probability events. Also thanks to Donald Fishbein who, over dinner in Paris with Brad, brainstormed the book's title, and to our diligent and excellent editors Lily O'Brien and Deborah Bancroft,—their keen eye for detail has relieved our manuscript of egregious grammatical flaws. David Brown helped us build a stunning website: *www.extreme-decisions.com.*

We are also indebted to people who read drafts of this book. This includes Kate Walters who braved reading an early draft of the book on a beach in Portugal and wrote, *"Despite the heat I have found myself shivering while following the travails of the frostbitten and half-starved . . ."* Her enthusiasm for the book spurred our desire to complete it to the best of our abilities.

Also we are grateful to Bob Headland, Kevin Kenny, Judy Skelton, Michael Smith, Rob Stephenson, and David Wilson, all of whom are leading experts in Antarctic history, for their in-depth critique of the manuscript.

Thanks also to our families and close friends who, for over a year, listened patiently while we regaled them (a few of whom might say "too many times") with tales of heroism and courage from the heroic age as we shaped our ideas for the book. The authors are most deeply indebted—Brad to his wife, Anne and daughter Brittany, and David to the light of his life, Alice Cochran—for their unflagging support and encouragement.

While we gained valuable insights from all the organizations and people named above, any errors within the book are our own.

Notes about the photographs

The photograph on this book's cover shows the severe hardship of man-hauling a heavily loaded sledge, especially on deep soft snow. Imagine doing this for mile after mile in freezing conditions, on limited food. Other than the sheer physical strain of doing this, one thing to be aware of is that even in Antarctica, physical exertion like this causes sweat, and as soon as the men would stop, the sweat would freeze on their bodies. Today in the comfort of our homes, one can only envision the degree of discomfort that would cause.

The photograph is from Scott's *Terra Nova* Expedition and was taken on December 13, 1911. It shows the Bowers sledge party. The men pulling the sledge using harnesses are, from left to right, Apsley Cherry-Garrard, Birdie Bowers, Patrick Keohane and Tom Crean. Dr. Edward Wilson is pushing on the sledge from the far side. The shape of his head and one of his shoulders are barely visible. Captain Robert Scott is the person whose back is to the camera pushing the sledge. It is believed that this photo was taken by Scott using a string to pull the shutter.

In this photograph, they are trying to drag the sledge through deep snow into the tracks created earlier by Lt. Evans' sledge party. The tracks lead towards the Beardmore Glacier.

The information about this photograph is based on correspondence with David Wilson. The reference is: *A Revised Illustrated Catalogue of Captain Scott's Photographs: 2016*, David M. Wilson, (ISBN: 978-0-901021-27-4), published by the Scott Polar Research Institute, © 2016

Use of this photograph was obtained from the Scott Polar Research Institute.

The stylized pictures at the start of each chapter were created using either contemporary photographs kindly provided for our use by friends, or historic photographs as noted below.

It's Your Call: Photograph by Joan Boothe
Chapter 1: Based on Herbert Ponting's photograph from Part III of *To the South Pole, Captain Scott's Own Story Told from his Journals. Strand Magazine*, 1913

Chapter 2: Photographic montage of images by Katie Murray and Rob Stephenson

Chapter 3: Based on a photograph by Robert Scott that appeared in *The Great White South* by Herbert Ponting, 1923 edition

Chapter 4: Composite image crafted from a photograph by Joan Boothe and a photograph by Herbert Ponting that appeared in *Scott's Last Expedition*, 1913 edition

Chapter 5: Based on a photograph by Herbert Ponting that appeared in *The Great White South* 1923 edition

Chapter 6: Based on a photograph by Herbert Ponting that appeared in *The Great White South* 1923 edition

Chapter 7: Photograph by Katie Murray

Chapter 8: Photograph by Vijay Samalam

Chapter 9: Photograph by Katie Murray

Chapter 10: Based on a photograph by Herbert Ponting that appeared in *The Great White South* 1923 edition

Chapter 11: Photograph by Katie Murray

Chapter 12: Photograph by Valerie Kerr

Postscript: Photograph by Vijay Samalam

About the authors

Brad Borkan has a graduate degree in Decision Sciences from the University of Pennsylvania where he co-authored two books on decision making with a Wharton professor. His twenty years with leading software companies has focused on helping large organizations improve their decision processes.

David Hirzel has written a three-part polar biography of the Irish explorer Tom Crean, a key player in Scott's and Shackleton's expeditions. The final book of this series, *Antarctic Voyager*, was launched at the South-Polesium conference in Scotland (May 2015). *Sailor on Ice: Tom Crean with Scott in the Antarctic* has been optioned for a documentary.

Business decision workshops and public speaking

The authors are both experienced public speakers and available to give presentations, and lead discussions and workshops on the decision topics in this book. These can focus on business decision making, personal decision making, or both.

For more details and for contact information, please see the authors' website: *www.extreme-decisions.com*

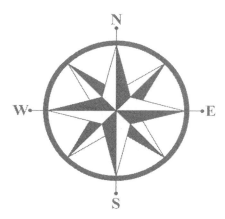

41178992R00115

Made in the USA
Middletown, DE
04 April 2019